DOCTOR JOHNSON
and his world

DOCTOR JOHNSON
and his world

BY F. E. HALLIDAY

A STUDIO BOOK

THE VIKING PRESS · NEW YORK

For Benedict and Kate, one of these days

I first read Boswell's *Life of Johnson* as an undergraduate, more than forty years ago. Since then it has been my constant bedside and breakfast-table book. Boswell led me to the memoirs of Mrs Thrale and Fanny Burney, and, of course, the works of Johnson himself. I can only hope that this book, with its illustrations, will introduce many readers besides Benedict and Kate to a similar lifelong delight.

St Ives
Cornwall
1967

F.E.H.

Lichfield. 'Its inhabitants are more orthodox in their religion, more pure in their language, and more polite in their manners, than those of any other town in the kingdom.'

THE PERIOD 1750–1780 IS KNOWN as the Age of Johnson, yet of all famous writers there can be few whose work is so little read today. As a poet Johnson was surpassed by Gray, as a dramatist by Goldsmith and Sheridan, as a novelist by Fielding and Sterne. Most readers know *The Elegy in a Country Churchyard, She Stoops to Conquer, The School for Scandal, The Vicar of Wakefield, Tom Jones* and *Tristram Shandy*, all written in the Age of Johnson; but how many have read *The Vanity of Human Wishes, Irene, Rasselas, The Rambler*, or consulted the definitions of his Dictionary? As a writer, a moralist in a mannered style, he was of his age, but as a man he was for all time: the man who is revealed in the pages of Boswell and, more endearingly, of Fanny Burney and Hester Thrale, but above all in his own works, which, until recently, have been so undeservedly neglected. Despite his poverty, constitutional melancholy and physical handicaps, by his courage and innate goodness, by his honesty, humanity, force of personality and manly vigour of conversation, he so dominated his age that even today we think of those thirty years from *The Rambler* to *The Lives of the Poets* as the Age of Johnson.

Samuel Johnson was born at Lichfield, some fifteen miles north of Birmingham, on 18 September 1709. At this time, before the beginning of the Industrial Revolution, Lichfield was a pleasant little town of some three thousand inhabitants, surrounded by open country, and divided into two unequal parts

Lichfield

5

Michael Johnson (1656–1731). 'A man of a large and robust body, and of a strong and active mind. Yet from him his son inherited "a vile melancholy".' (*Boswell*)

Johnson's birthplace, and St Mary's Church, where he was baptized on the day of his birth, 18 September 1709.

by the Minster Pool. On the south lay the town proper, the shops and houses of the burgesses, and on the north were the Cathedral and Close. 'In the first,' wrote Daniel Defoe, 'is the Market Place, a fine school and a very handsome hospital. . . . This part is much the larger and the most populous: but the other is the fairest, and has the best buildings in it, and, among the rest, the Cathedral Church, one of the finest and most beautiful in England. . . . There are in the Close, besides the houses of the Clergy Residentiaries, a great number of well-built and well-inhabited houses; which made Lichfield a place of good company, above all the towns in this or the neighbouring counties.'

It was in the Market Place that Samuel's father, Michael Johnson, built a substantial house and shop after his marriage with Sarah Ford in 1706. He was a self-made man of fifty, who had established himself in Lichfield as a book-seller twenty-five years before, and taken a prominent part in local affairs, being

◄ Lichfield Cathedral. It was more severely damaged than any other during the Civil War and Commonwealth.

The Stuarts encouraged the custom of touching for the 'King's Evil', as proof of their Divine Right. The Hanoverians refused, and Queen Anne was the last to touch.

To the Kings most Excellent Majesty.

The Humble

PETITION

Of divers hundreds

Of the Kings poore Subjects,

Afflicted with that grievous Infirmitie,

CALLED

The Kings Evill.

Of which by his Majesties absence they have no possibility of being cured, wanting all meanes to gaine accesse to his Majesty, by reason of His abode at OXFORD.

London, Printed for *John Wilkinson.*
*Febr.*20. *Anno Dom.* 1643.   1642

The Tory attempt to restore the Stuarts in 1715, when Johnson was six, was easily defeated by the Whig government.

Queen Anne, last of the Stuarts (1702–14).

George I, first of the Hanoverians (1714–27).

Sheriff in the year of Sam's birth: a tall, strong but melancholy man, a High Churchman and a Tory. Political opinions were of some moment in those last years of Queen Anne's reign, the age of Addison and Steele, *The Spectator* and *The Tatler*, of Marlborough's victorious campaigns, then of the establishment of the Hanoverian George I by the Whigs in 1714, and the first Jacobite attempt to restore the Stuarts in 1715.

Sarah Ford, a spinster of thirty-seven when she married, belonged to a higher social class than her husband. Her father was a small landowner, many of her relations were professional men, and some connected by marriage with the gentry. Although she did not share Michael's interest in books, she was said to be a woman of remarkable understanding.

Johnson wrote a short account of the first ten years of his life. His mother, aged forty when he, her first child, was born, had a difficult and dangerous labour. 'I was born half dead,' he wrote, and his chances of survival seemed so slight that he was christened on the same day. Yet the child lived, and was placed with a wet-nurse, from whom he returned two months later, 'a poor diseased infant, almost blind', infected with scrofula and deaf in his left ear. The superstition still lingered that scrofula, the 'King's Evil', could be cured by the royal touch, and when he was two his mother took him to be touched by Queen Anne. He retained a confused memory of a lady in a black hood, and

9

though she performed no miracle that day, for the rest of his life he wore the gold charm that she had hung round his neck. As another memento, his mother bought him a small silver spoon and cup, marked 'Sam. J.'. She was pregnant again, and soon after Sam's third birthday her second and last child, Nathaniel, was born.

'My father and mother had not much happiness from each other.' They seldom conversed, for they had little in common, though Sarah liked to talk about her grand relations, and belittle Michael's: his brother Andrew, for example, an unsuccessful Birmingham bookseller, and former champion boxer, who was, apparently, to teach Sam the art. The Johnsons, like the Fords, were all big and physically strong.

When the domestic atmosphere became over-strained, Michael would take his horse and ride away in search of orders, leaving his young son to be taught by his mother. 'I remember that, being in bed with my mother one morning, I was told by her of the two places to which the inhabitants of this world were received after death: one a fine place filled with happiness, called heaven, the other a *sad* place, called hell. That this account much affected my imagination, I do not remember.' It may well be, however, that this was the source of his constant terror of death: 'So much so,' he said sixty years later, 'that the whole of life is but keeping away the thought of it.'

Sam loved his mother – 'My dear mother', he always called her – though he could not respect her, and though he had some respect for his father, he could not love him. Michael was too old and remote, 'a foolish old man' who angered the child by making him display his precocity. For Sam was very precocious, and one day, when he could just read, memorized the Collect that his mother had given him to learn, while she was climbing the stairs.

His quick temper is illustrated by an incident that happened while he was learning to read at Dame Oliver's school. It was little more than a hundred yards away, but he was so short-sighted that a servant used to fetch him home. Once, however, he set off by himself, groping on hands and knees to find the gutter before crossing the road, and when his schoolmistress followed him, he felt it such an insult to his independence that he ran at her and beat her.

The schoolboy From dame school he graduated to another little school kept by Tom Brown, a shoemaker, immortalized as the author of a spelling-book that he dedicated to the Universe. Then, at the age of seven, he entered Lichfield Grammar School. It was a good school, with a distinguished list of old boys, and there the grossly underpaid usher Humphrey Hawkins introduced him to Latin, virtually the only subject taught in those days. After two years with the gentle Hawkins, he moved into the upper school under the headmaster, John Hunter, a sound scholar but shaky psychologist, who believed that Latin could be

Lichfield Grammar School, which Johnson attended between the ages of seven and sixteen.

whipped into his pupils. He was more than severe, he was brutal, 'so brutal that no man who had been educated by him ever sent his son to the same school.' Not that Johnson disapproved of the rod, but he did disapprove of Hunter's wrong-headed severity. The boy was indolent, but had a prodigious memory, so that learning came easily, and he was able to help his companions, some of whom, in gratitude, would carry him to school in the morning. One of these was Edmund Hector, and another contemporary was John Taylor, a boarder from Ashbourne. Both of them were to remain his lifelong friends.

He was too big for his age, too clumsy and short-sighted to play games, but he liked sliding in winter, or, better still, being pulled along the ice by another boy. In summer his father taught him to swim in the neighbouring Stowe Pool, or he would wander about the fields with Hector, talking, though usually to himself. Then, at home, in his father's shop, there was an unlimited supply of books. And he began to write poetry.

Johnson's cousin, Parson Ford, stirring the punch. 'He was a man of great parts, very profligate, but I never heard he was impious.' He died in 1731.

In 1725 Michael Johnson was elected Senior Bailiff. He was sixty-six, however, his powers were failing, his affairs in a muddle, and Sarah's nephew and trustee, Cornelius Ford, came to make new arrangements about her dowry. Sam was just sixteen, his cousin twice his age: a former Cambridge don, companion of poets, acquainted with the best society in London, a rake who had recently repaired his fortune by marrying a minor heiress and taking holy orders. Sam was enchanted, and Cornelius invited him to his home at Pedmore, near Stourbridge. It.was to have been a short visit, but Sam stayed six months, absorbing the scholarship and reminiscences of Cornelius, and learning the art of conversation. 'Obtain,' said the worldly parson, 'some general principles of every science; he who can talk only on one subject is seldom wanted.' Sam remembered his advice, but when he returned to Lichfield in the early summer of 1726, Hunter refused to have the truant back at school. Cornelius came to the rescue, and he spent the rest of the year at Stourbridge Grammar School.

He was now seventeen, and had there been money enough he would have gone to the university. As it was, he had to resign himself to helping in the shop, learning to bind books and tan hides in his father's parchment factory. But Michael Johnson & Son was a tottering concern; Sam preferred reading books to selling them, and even refused to go to Uttoxeter to manage their stall when his father was ill, an unkindness for which he did penance in old age, by standing for an hour in Uttoxeter market place, bareheaded in the rain.

He found some consolation in the company of Gilbert Walmesley, a cathedral official who lived in the Bishop's Palace. Like Cornelius Ford, Walmesley was a scholar and reformed rake, though, unlike Cornelius, permanently reformed. Now a benevolent bachelor of fifty, he befriended the ungainly, frustrated youth, invited him to the Palace, argued with him – he was as violent a Whig as Sam a Tory – and introduced him to Lichfield society, including the family of Captain Garrick, whose third son David was another of his favourites. Although David was eight years younger than Sam, he was talented and vivacious, a brilliant mimic, and the two became friends.

The Bishop's Palace, Lichfield, where Gilbert Walmesley, Registrar of the Ecclesiastical Court, lived. He died in 1751. 'It may be doubted whether a day now passes, in which I have not some advantage from his friendship.'

In 1728 Sam's prospects brightened. His mother received a legacy of £40 from one of her wealthy relations, and seems to have invested the money in her elder son's further education. So, in October, when just nineteen, he entered Pembroke College, Oxford, as a commoner. The immense range of his knowledge, acquired by avid and desultory reading, astonished his teachers, and he himself admitted that he knew as much Latin at eighteen as he did at sixty. According to one of the Junior Fellows, William Adams, he was 'a gay and frolicsome' undergraduate, loved by all about him; but gaiety was only a cloak for his unhappiness. 'I was rude and violent,' he protested in later life. 'It was bitterness that they mistook for frolic. I was miserably poor, and I thought to fight my way by my literature and my wit; so I disregarded all power and authority.' He cut lectures, was rude to his Tutor, failed to present his work,

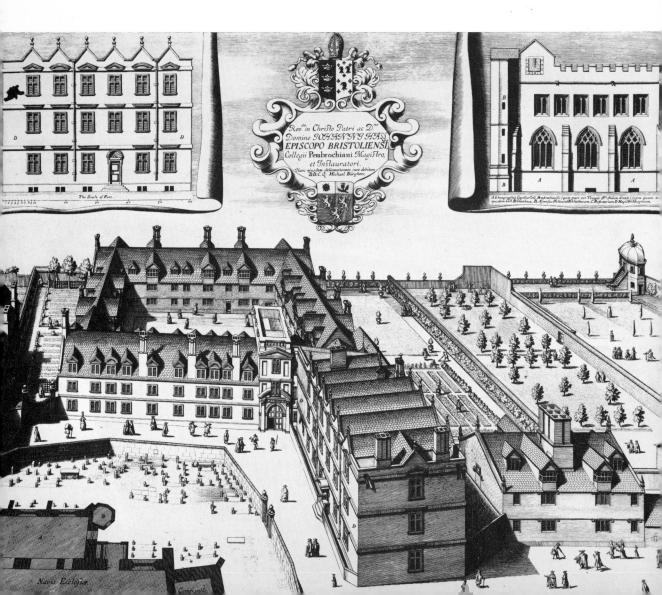

and would lounge about the college gates entertaining his comrades with his wit. His rediscovery of religion, which for some time he had neglected, may have intensified his unhappiness, for after reading William Law's *Serious Call to a Devout and Holy Life*, the fear of death, hell and damnation obsessed him, and in the late summer of 1729 he was attacked by the acute melancholia that was to torment him for the rest of his life. It was now that he developed the odd, convulsive movements that became so characteristic.

He was as proud as he was poor, and when his shoes wore out, and somebody placed a new pair by his door, he threw them indignantly away. His money was exhausted, and in December he 'hid his toes in a pair of large boots', and set off for Lichfield to see if his parents could help him further. It was to be twenty-five years before he returned to Oxford.

Pembroke College, Oxford. Johnson's room was the top one above the gateway. 'Johnson was peculiarly happy in mentioning how many of the sons of Pembroke were poets . . . "Sir, we were a nest of singing birds." ' (*Boswell*)

Birmingham *c.* 1733. 'He made some valuable acquaintances there, amongst whom were Mr Porter, a mercer, whose widow he afterwards married. . . . But the comfort of being

Despondency Johnson found his father's parchment factory falling to pieces for lack of money to repair it, and there could be no question of further funds to keep him at Oxford. He had been there little more than a year, and now, an ambitious young man of twenty, conscious of his powers, he found himself without a degree, without money, without prospects, handicapped by partial blindness and deafness, disfigured by scrofula and smallpox. No wonder he sank into a morbid melancholy, and even feared the loss of what he valued most, his reason. In an attempt to overcome his mental disorder he frequently walked to Birmingham, where in desperation he consulted his godfather, Dr Swinfen, giving him an account of his case, written in Latin, which Swinfen proudly but foolishly showed to his friends.

At Lichfield he found some relief at the Palace with Walmesley, who introduced him to a son of the Earl of Bristol, Henry Hervey, a lively young officer who wrote verses to young ladies. Johnson emulated him, among the girls whom he celebrated being 'Stella', Dorothy Hickman of Stourbridge, a distant

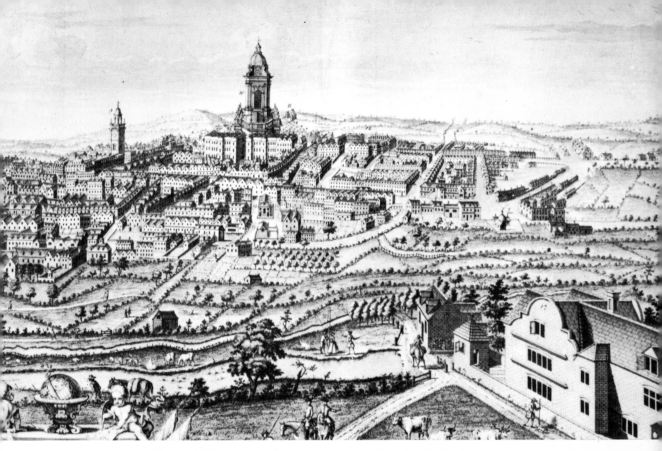

near Mr Hector, his old school-fellow and intimate friend, was Johnson's chief inducement to continue here.' (*Boswell*)

cousin. This was when he applied for the post of usher at Stourbridge Grammar School. He failed. He had no degree.

In December 1731 his father died, leaving little but his house and bookshop, which his mother and brother Nathaniel prepared to carry on, and in the following spring he set out for Market Bosworth, where he had been accepted as usher at the grammar school. He loathed the unimaginative drudgery, as well as the patron of the school, Sir Wolstan Dixie, a boorish young baronet who made him act as a kind of domestic chaplain, and when he found that he had inherited £20 from his father's estate, the equivalent of a year's salary, he resigned in disgust and returned to Lichfield. 'I have my fortune to make,' he noted in Latin, 'and must take care that in the meantime the powers of my mind do not grow languid through poverty, nor want drive me into wickedness.' After another unsuccessful attempt to get a job as schoolmaster, this time at Ashbourne, where John Taylor lived, he received an invitation to stay with his other school friend, Edmund Hector, now a young surgeon in Birmingham.

It was to be a protracted and momentous visit. Among the friends to whom Hector introduced Johnson was the mercer Henry Porter, his wife Elizabeth, and their children, two boys and their elder sister Lucy, aged about seventeen. Johnson was attracted by the fresh-complexioned, pretty Lucy, though her description of the young man was by no means flattering: 'He was then lean and lank, so that his immense structure of bones was hideously striking to the eye, and the scars of the scrofula were deeply visible. He also wore his hair, which was straight and stiff, separated behind; and he often had seemingly convulsive starts and odd gesticulations, which tended to excite at once surprise and ridicule.' It was not Lucy, but her mother who remarked of their wild-eyed visitor, 'This is the most sensible man that I ever saw in my life.'

Hector did his best to dispel his friend's melancholy. Sometimes they drank too much, but that seems to have been the limit of their dissipation, and Hector persuaded Johnson to begin translating a French version of a Portuguese book about Abyssinia. It was one thing to begin, another to continue, and such was Johnson's indolence that Hector himself wrote the last part to the dictation of Johnson as he lay in bed. *A Voyage to Abyssinia*, Johnson's first book, for which he received five guineas, was published anonymously in 1735.

He had returned to Lichfield before this, where he contemplated an edition of the Latin poems of Politian, and wrote to Edward Cave, proprietor of the recently founded literary periodical *The Gentleman's Magazine*, suggesting that he might become a contributor, and even offering advice. Then, in September 1734 came the news of Henry Porter's death. Johnson returned to Birmingham to console the widow, and within a year they were married. He was twenty-five, his bride forty-six.

Johnson's wife, Tetty – 'Pretty charmer!' ▶

Marriage Bond given by Samuel Johnson, 8 July 1735, on applying for a licence to marry Mrs Elizabeth Porter.

Samuel Johnson. The earliest-known portrait.

𝕿𝖍𝖊 𝕮𝖔𝖓𝖉𝖎𝖙𝖎𝖔𝖓 of the above-written Obligation is such, That if there shall not hereafter appear any lawful Let or Impediment, by reason of any Pre-Contract, Consanguinity, Affinity, or any other just Cause whatsoever; but that *Samuel Johnson of the Parish of Saint Mary in Lichfield in the County of Stafford Bachelor Aged twenty five Years Gentleman And Elizabeth Porter of the Parish of Saint Philip in Birmingham in the County of Warwick Widow Aged forty Years* _____

may lawfully marry together: And that there is not any Suit depending before any Judge Ecclesiastical or Civil, for, or concerning any such Pre-Contract: And that the Consent of the Parents, or others the Governors of the said Parties, be thereunto first had and obtain'd; And that they cause their said Marriage to be openly solemnized in the Face of the Parish Church of *Saint Philip in Birmingham or Saint Werburgh in Derby* _____ between the Hours of Eight and Twelve of the Clock in the Forenoon; And do and shall save harmless and keep indemnified the abovenam'd *Richard Rider* _____ his Surrogates, and all others his Officers, and Successors in Office, for, and concerning the Premises:
Then the said Obligation to be void; or else to be and remain in full Force and Virtue.

Sealed and Delivered (being first duly stamped) in the Presence of

Garrick's later description of the former Mrs Elizabeth Porter, 'Tetty', as Johnson affectionately called her, should not be taken too seriously: 'very fat, with a bosom of more than ordinary protuberance, with swelled cheeks of a florid red, produced by thick painting, and increased by the liberal use of cordials; flaring and fantastic in her dress, and affected both in her speech and her general behaviour'. Garrick was much given to caricature, it was his profession, and, whatever she may have become in later years, his description bears no resemblance to the portrait painted when she was a younger woman. Johnson could make himself very agreeable to women of all ages, and Tetty was fascinated by his intelligence and conversation, and no doubt there was something maternal in her love. As for Johnson, he was desperately in need of comfort and love, of the kind of love that only an older, understanding woman could give. The fact that she had a fortune of £600 did not make her less attractive, but Johnson was the least mercenary of men, and certainly did not marry for money. 'It was a love-match on both sides,' he always insisted, and there is every reason to believe him.

As their marriage was disapproved of by both families, they were married in Derby, in St Werburgh's Church, on 9 July 1735. As they rode north, Tetty complained that her lover went too fast, then too slowly, until to teach her a lesson and who was master, he rode ahead and out of sight; then waited. When she came up with him, she was in tears. The tamer was tamed, and it was he who, on the anniversary of her death seventeen years later, was to be reduced to tears.

He made another attempt to secure a teaching post, this time the head-mastership of the school at Solihull, then a village near Birmingham, but the governors replied that, though he was known to be an excellent scholar, 'he has the Caracter of being a very haughty ill natured Gent, & that he has such a way of distorting his Face (which though he can't help) the Gent. think it may affect some Young Ladds.' Perhaps they had heard the story of Johnson's encounter with a man who took his chair in the wings of the stage during the performance of a play in Lichfield Guildhall. When the man refused to surrender his seat, Johnson tossed him, chair and all, into the pit.

He now embarked on a scheme that he had been considering for some time: his own academy for young gentlemen. The money was Tetty's, and, helped by Walmesley, he rented a large house at Edial, near Lichfield, and by the beginning of 1736 he had half a dozen boarders, including David Garrick and his brother George. There was no chance of its succeeding. Johnson was no schoolmaster: his own vast knowledge had been acquired by desultory reading, tearing the essence out of books without perusing from beginning to end; he disliked routine, and was the last man to make his pupils study systematically.

Johnson advertises in *The Gentleman's Magazine*, June/July 1736.

ADVERTISEMENTS.

A T Edial, near *Litchfield* in *Stafford-shire*, Young Gentlemen are Boarded, and Taught the *Latin* and *Greek* Languages, by   Samuel Johnson.

Edial Academy, where Johnson taught David Garrick and other Young Gentlemen in 1736.

'Mr Johnson to try his Fate with a Tragedy.' Gilbert Walmesley's letter of introduction to the Rev. Mr Colson.

Then, the Solihull gents were right: the lads had no reverence for their young master; they laughed at his uncouth gesticulations, and peeped through his bedroom keyhole to watch his 'tumultuous and awkward fondness' for Tetty. No more pupils came, some of the old ones left, and by the autumn he was applying for another post as assistant master, only to be rejected again because his mannerisms 'might become the object of imitation or of ridicule among his pupils'.

He had nothing to hope from schoolmastering. In the seven years that had elapsed since he left Oxford, his only employment had been the four miserable months at Market Bosworth, and now his own short-lived academy was on the verge of collapse, involving the loss of most of Tetty's fortune. His real ambition was to write, and as the best way to succeed was to write a successful play, he began the blank-verse tragedy of *Irene*, a Turkish tale. When finished, it would have to be produced in London, and as David Garrick was to go there on his way to another academy, they decided to travel together. Edial Academy was closed, and on 2 March 1737, like Shakespeare and Marlowe a hundred and fifty years before, Johnson set off for London to make his fortune as a dramatist. Tetty and Lucy remained in Lichfield, and Walmesley wrote to Garrick's new headmaster, recommending both 'this young gentleman' and 'another neighbour of mine, one Mr Samuel Johnson . . . a very good scholar and poet, and I have great hopes will turn out a fine tragedy-writer'.

The London of 1737 was a city of fine buildings, from medieval Westminster to Wren's new St Paul's Cathedral and steepled churches by the river. It was also a city of squalor and brutality, of open sewers and rotting offal in unswept streets, of robbery and murder in unlighted alleys, the city of Gin Lane and public hangings at Tyburn, as depicted by Hogarth. The drama was moribund, and polite society frequented the Italian operas of Handel, less polite society *The Beggar's Opera* of Gay. Pope, the literary lion of the day, lived in affluence at Twickenham, but most aspiring writers starved in Grub Street, or earned a pittance by writing political pamphlets for Walpole and the Whigs, or for their Tory opponents, or both. Johnson, the Lichfield boy, had never experienced anything like this vast, teeming London. It needed courage for a married man of twenty-seven to try to make his fortune there by writing; but nobody ever accused Johnson of lack of courage.

He found lodgings in Exeter Street, near the Strand, and dined on bread, meat and water at a neighbouring tavern for eightpence, which included a penny tip for the waiter. But even in London Walmesley could help. He had recently married Magdalen Aston, sister of Henry Hervey's wife, and as the Herveys were living in London, they often asked Johnson to dinner. 'He was a vicious man,' Johnson told Boswell, 'but very kind to me. If you call a dog Hervey, I shall love him.'

His business, however, was to finish *Irene*, and he left the noise and bustle of Fleet Street for the rural quiet of Greenwich, where he composed the speeches while walking in the park. This was a customary mode of composition, and sometimes he would have as many as fifty lines of verse in his head before writing them down, an exercise of memory that must have contributed to the ease, accuracy and force of his conversation.

In the autumn, partly perhaps because of the death of his brother, he went back to Lichfield. Nathaniel had been a wild, noisy young man, who got into some sort of trouble, deserted his mother and the bookshop, and died soon after a prodigal's return, and Sam's departure for London. Johnson stayed in Lichfield long enough to finish his tragedy and settle his affairs; then, having arranged for Lucy to stay with his mother and help with the bookshop, he returned to London with Tetty, to new lodgings near Hanover Square.

David Garrick's elder brother Peter was in town, and as he knew the manager of Drury Lane Theatre, he introduced Johnson with his tragedy. It was no use. London theatre managers were not interested in blank-verse plays by unknown authors, and *Irene* remained unacted, probably unread.

Now that his last and most precious hope had failed, Johnson's only resource was Grub Street journalism, and again he approached Edward Cave of *The Gentleman's Magazine*, which for the next six years was to be his principal source

London when Johnson arrived in 1737.

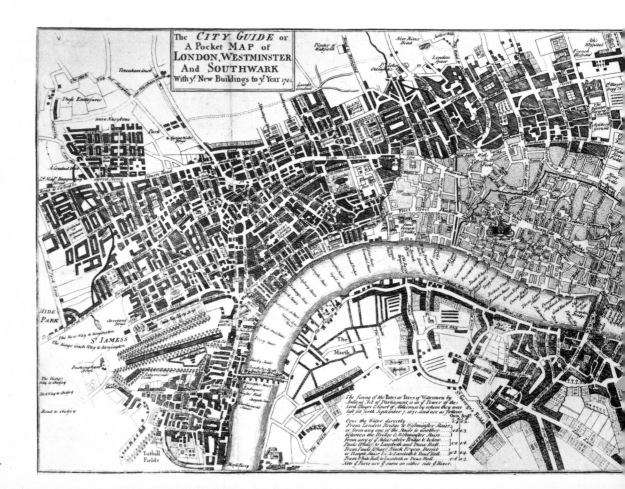

A Tyburn hanging. 'Sir, executions are intended to draw spectators. If they do not draw spectators, they don't answer their purpose.'

Gin Lane.

Irene. 'A few days before his death, while burning a great mass of papers, he picked out from among them the original unformed sketch of this tragedy, in his own hand-writing. . . . It contains fragments of the intended plot, and speeches for the different persons of the drama, partly in the raw materials of prose, partly worked up into verse.'
(*Boswell*)

Greenwich Park, where Johnson composed part of *Irene* in 1737.

Edward Cave, founder of *The Gentleman's Magazine*, 1731. 'His resolution and perseverance were very uncommon.'

Johnson's first contribution: *On Mr Urban's Adversaries*. 'He told me that, when he first saw St John's Gate, he beheld it with reverence.' (*Boswell*)

of income. Cave, slow but shrewd, was impressed by the young man, whose first contribution appeared in March 1738: a Latin poem to 'Sylvanus Urban', Cave's pseudonym. Soon afterwards he wrote to Cave, enclosing a poem by 'an author' who 'lies at present under very disadvantageous circumstances of fortune'. The author was Johnson himself, the poem *London*. It was published anonymously by Cave and Robert Dodsley in May. Johnson received ten guineas for the copyright.

London, an imitation of Juvenal's satire on the abuses of ancient Rome, is the poem of a young man disillusioned by the city in which he had hoped to find recognition, and embittered by his failure:

> *This mournful truth is every where confess'd:*
> SLOW RISES WORTH BY POVERTY DEPRESS'D.

It is also an attack on the government of Walpole, and in the sententious couplets many of Johnson's prejudices appear – excise, pensioners, foreigners, a standing army:

> *Ere masquerades debauch'd, excise depress'd,*
> *Or English honour grew a standing jest . . .*
> *Here let those reign whom pensions can incite*
> *To vote a patriot black, a courtier white . . .*
> *London, the needy villain's general home,*
> *The common-sewer of Paris and of Rome!*

The poem was a great success; a second edition was printed within a week, and even Pope pronounced that 'the author, whoever he may be, will not long be concealed'.

But Johnson could not live for long on praise and ten guineas, and in his Castle Street lodgings he drudged away at translations and other contributions for Cave's magazine. He also wrote an entertaining satire in the manner of Swift: *Marmor Norfolciense*. According to this, in Norfolk, Walpole's county, a stone with an old inscription is discovered:

Grub Street. 'Originally the name of a street in Moorfields in London, much inhabited by writers of small histories, dictionaries, and temporary poems.'

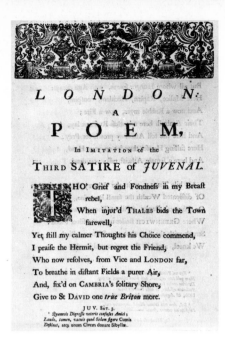

Whene'er this stone, now hid beneath the lake,
The horse shall trample, or the plough shall break,
Then, O my country! shalt thou groan distrest,
Grief swell thine eyes, and terror chill thy breast . . .
Then thro' thy fields shall scarlet reptiles stray,
And rapine and pollution mark their way. . . .

An ingenuous antiquary tries to interpret the inscription: 'The lake is dry, the stone is turned up, but there is no appearance of this dismal scene. Is not all at home satisfaction and tranquillity? . . . and are we not secured by a numerous standing army?' What, then, can be the meaning of 'scarlet reptiles'? Can it be a reference to the plague of lady-birds in Kent? It is excellent, written with a rare lightness of touch.

Johnson himself can have been in no light-hearted mood. He was miserably poor, sometimes living on fourpence-halfpenny a day, and one of his letters to Cave is signed 'Yours *impransus*', that is, 'without breakfast'. He had found a friend among the other impecunious contributors to the magazine, Richard Savage, an improvident poet twelve years his senior, and when they could not pay for a bed they wandered together whole nights in the streets. Even the little silver cup that Johnson's mother had given him as a child was sold: 'one of the last pieces of plate which dear Tetty sold, in our distress'. Where she was at this time is not clear. Perhaps Johnson could just afford a comfortable lodging for her, while he walked the streets, or slept in cellars with Savage. Or perhaps there had been a temporary estrangement: Tetty was houseproud and neat,

Richard Savage

29

Johnson incurably untidy and given to chemical experiments, and they may well have got on one another's nerves.

In July 1739 Savage parted from Johnson with tears in his eyes, and set off for Wales, and soon afterwards Johnson set off for Leicestershire. There was another chance of a headmastership. Pope, who knew Johnson merely as the author of *London*, generously tried to get him an MA degree from Trinity College, Dublin, but his application failed, as therefore did Johnson's. A headmaster must have a degree.

He was in need of a holiday, and lingered for some months in the Midlands. He stayed with Taylor at Ashbourne, where he was entertained by the gentry, and began his friendship with the 'methodistic' Miss Hill Boothby. In Lichfield he found metal even more attractive in Walmesley's sister-in-law, Molly Aston. 'I wonder when anybody ever experiences measureless delight?' he was to ask later. 'I never did, I'm sure, except the first evening I spent tête-à-tête with Molly Aston.' Not unnaturally Tetty was jealous of the Lichfield siren, but when, at the beginning of 1740, Johnson heard that she had hurt her leg, he wrote to her repentantly: 'I still promise myself many happy years from your tenderness and affection, which I sometimes hope our misfortunes have not yet deprived me of.' He and his mother then mortgaged the house and bookshop for £80, from his share of which he was able to send £20 to Tetty before leaving Lichfield some weeks later. It was to be another twenty years before he saw the town again.

He was back in London early in 1740, and began another four years' drudgery for *The Gentleman's Magazine*, to which he now became the main contributor. In addition to the usual articles, translations and occasional verses, he wrote short lives of famous English sailors, Sir Francis Drake and Admiral Blake, early essays in biography that proved popular now that England was again at war. He also took over the reporting of parliamentary debates. Strictly speaking, this was forbidden, but Cave and Johnson got over the difficulty by reporting what they called the Senate of Lilliput, the speakers of which were given fictitious names. Johnson himself did not attend debates, and had only a few notes to work from, but these he expanded into imaginary orations, always taking care that 'the Whig dogs should not have the best of it'.

Although constitutionally lazy, Johnson was a very rapid writer once he had begun; the matter was all in his head, neatly arranged, and it was merely a question of transcription. He could write twenty columns of the magazine in an afternoon, and he had, therefore, time for other literary activities. Always interested in medicine and chemistry, he helped to compile a *Medicinal Dictionary*, and was employed by its publisher, Thomas Osborne, to catalogue the famous library of Edward Harley, Earl of Oxford, which Osborne had

Johnson reconstructs a speech made in the Commons by William Pitt. 'He said that the Parliamentary Debates were the only part of his writings which then gave him any compunction: but that at the time he wrote them he had no conception he was imposing upon the world, though they were frequently written from very slender materials, often from none at all – the mere coinage of his own imagination.' (*Boswell*)

Petulancy of Invectives, contribute to the Purposes for which this Assembly is called together; how little the Discovery of Truth is promoted, and the Security of the Nation established by pompous Diction, and theatrical Emotions.

Formidable Sounds, and furious Declamations, confident Assertions, and lofty Periods, may affect the young and unexperienced, and perhaps the Gentleman may have contracted his Habits of Oratory by conversing more with those of his own Age, than with such as have had more Opportunities of acquiring Knowledge, and more successful Methods of communicating their Sentiments.

If the Heat of his Temper, Sir, would suffer him to attend to those whose Age and long Acquaintance with Business, give them an indisputable Right to Deference and Superiority, he would learn, in Time, to reason rather than declaim, and to prefer Justness of Argument, and an accurate Knowledge of Facts, to founding Epithets and splendid Superlatives, which may disturb the Imagination for a Moment, but leave no lasting Impression on the Mind.

He will learn, Sir, that to accuse and prove are very different, and that Reproaches unsupported by Evidence, affect only the Character of him that utters them. Excursions of Fancy, and Flights of Oratory, are indeed pardonable in young Men, but in no other; and it would surely contribute more, even to the Purpose for which some Gentlemen appear to speak, that of depreciating the Conduct of the Administration, to prove the Inconveniencies and Injustice of this Bill, than barely to assert them, with whatever Magnificence of Language, or Appearance of Zeal, Honesty, or Compassion.

The Urg: Ptit replied.

SIR,

THE atrocious Crime of being a young Man, which the honourable Gentleman has with such Spirit and Decency charged upon me, I shall neither attempt to palliate, nor deny, but content myself with wishing that I may be one of those whose Follies may cease with their Youth, and not of that Number, who are ignorant in spite of Experience.

Whether Youth can be imputed to any Man as a Reproach, I will not, Sir, assume the Province of determining; but surely Age may become justly contemptible, if the Opportunities which it brings have past away without Improvement, and Vice appears to prevail when the Passions have subsided. The Wretch that, after having seen the Consequences of a thousand Errors, continues still to blunder, and whose Age has only added Obstinacy to Stupidity, is surely the Object of either Abhorrence or Contempt, and deserves not that his grey Head should secure him from Insults.

Much more, Sir, is he to be abhorr'd, who, as he has advanced in Age, has receded from Virtue, and becomes more wicked with less Temptation; who prostitutes himself for Money which he cannot enjoy, and spends the Remains of his Life in the Ruin of his Country.

But Youth, Sir, is not my only Crime; I have been accused of acting a theatrical Part — A theatrical Part may either imply some Peculiarities of Gesture, or a Dissimulation of my real Sentiments, and an Adoption of the Opinions and Language of another Man.

In the first Sense, Sir, the Charge is too trifling to be confuted, and deserves only to be mentioned, that it may be despised. I am at Liberty, like every other Man, to use my own Language; and though I may perhaps have some Ambition to please this Gentleman, I shall not lay myself under any Restraint, nor very sollicitously copy his Diction, or his Mien, however matured by Age, or modelled by Experience.

If any Man shall by charging me with theatrical Behaviour imply, that I utter any Sentiments but my own, I shall treat him as a Calumniator, and a Villain;

bought. Osborne was a coarse, insolent man, and the story went that one day, irritated by the slowness of the work, he began to abuse Johnson, who, losing all patience, felled him with a folio and set his foot upon his breast. 'He was impertinent to me,' Johnson explained, 'and I beat him. But it was not in his shop: it was in my chamber.'

He also found time for a labour of love: to write the life of his friend Savage, who died in a Bristol jail in 1743. Savage, who claimed to be the illegitimate son of the Countess of Macclesfield, was an indifferent poet and a dissolute man, but Johnson was attracted by such sinners, provided they were professing Christians and showed signs of repentance: such men as Walmesley, Ford, Hervey – and Boswell. He did not attempt to conceal Savage's vices, but he also revealed his virtues, and his book is not only an apology for the man, but also an apology for man; and it set a new standard for biography.

The Life of Richard Savage was published in 1744, again without the author's name, and Johnson received fifteen guineas, twelve of which he owed as interest on the mortgage of the Lichfield house. He could not afford new clothes, and was so shabbily dressed that he refused to sit at table with Cave when he had guests, preferring to eat his dinner behind a screen. Such poverty must have been particularly galling when his former pupil, Garrick, was earning £500 a year as an actor. He had leaped into fame in 1741 in the part of Richard III, and was now the darling of Drury Lane. 'A fellow who claps a hump on his back, and a lump on his leg, and cries *I am Richard the Third*,' growled Johnson. He had an Elizabethan contempt for actors, 'mouthing words that better wits have framed;' but nobody else could abuse his Davy.

Perhaps it was Garrick's success in Shakespeare that goaded Johnson to greater efforts, to break away from hack-work and embark on some great project of his own, for in 1745 appeared his pamphlet, *Miscellaneous Observations on the*

◀ Garrick as Richard III, the part in which he made his name.

William Warburton (1698–1779), Bishop of Gloucester, who called Johnson's *Miscellaneous Observations on the Tragedy of Macbeth* the work of 'a man of parts and genius'. 'He praised me at a time when praise was of value to me.'

Tragedy of Macbeth, and *Proposals for Printing a new Edition of the Plays of Shakespear*. The *Observations* show Johnson's strength and weakness as an editor: his sturdy common sense, and his inadequate knowledge of Elizabethan language and literature. His was a great century for the editing of Shakespeare; three editors had already produced their texts, and while Johnson was writing, a fourth appeared, Sir Thomas Hanmer's, of which he mildly remarked, 'Its pomp recommends it more than its accuracy.' Yet another was on its way, William Warburton's, and for the time being Johnson abandoned his project.

This was the year of the Jacobite Rebellion, when Prince Charles Edward and his Highlanders invaded England, and Johnson with his Jacobite sympathies must have listened eagerly for news as they marched on Derby, only twenty-five miles from Lichfield. The rebellion ended disastrously at Culloden in April 1746, when Johnson was preparing to sign a contract with a group of publishers for *A Dictionary of the English Language*.

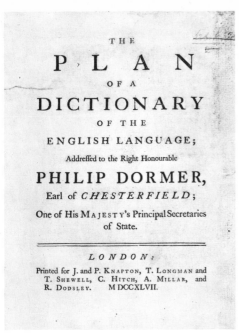

THE
PLAN
OF A
DICTIONARY
OF THE
ENGLISH LANGUAGE;

Addreſſed to the Right Honourable

PHILIP DORMER,

Earl of *CHESTERFIELD*;

One of His MAJESTY's Principal Secretaries
of State.

LONDON:

Printed for J. and P. KNAPTON, T. LONGMAN and
T. SHEWELL, C. HITCH, A. MILLAR, and
R. DODSLEY. MDCCXLVII.

The Plan
and the Patron

There were already English dictionaries, though there was none that did what Johnson proposed to do. In his *Plan of a Dictionary* he explained that his chief intent was 'to preserve the purity, and ascertain the meaning, of our English idiom'; that in addition to the spelling, pronunciation, etymology and definition of words, their use would be illustrated by quotations from the best authors. It was to be an anthology as well as a dictionary, and was to take three years. When his former college friend Dr Adams observed that it took the French Academy of forty members forty years to compile their Dictionary, Johnson replied: 'Let me see; forty times forty is sixteen hundred. As three to sixteen hundred, so is the proportion of an Englishman to a Frenchman.'

He now moved into a large house in Gough Square, Fleet Street, and *Gough Square* engaged six assistants for the work, which was carried out in the garret. The *Plan* was printed in 1747, and addressed to Lord Chesterfield, an elegant and cynical nobleman who gave Johnson £10, and became patron of the work. Unfortunately his interest was to wane as the years went by.

 17 Gough Square, Fleet Street, where Johnson lived 1748–58, while compiling his Dictionary.

Despite his brighter prospects, Johnson was not happy. Tetty was deteriorating. Now nearly sixty, she had taken to drink and drugs, refused to let her husband share her bed, and preferred to live in the country air of Hampstead while he toiled in the smoke of London. Johnson was a man of strong passions, and thus to be deprived of physical love while still in his thirties was an intolerable strain. But his principles were even stronger than his passions. When Tetty began to drink too much, he became an abstainer; and there was no question of other women, though when he went to Hampstead, almost in desperation he would fondle the young widow Elizabeth Desmoulins, Dr Swinfen's daughter, who lived with Tetty.

It was under these conditions, and largely at Hampstead, that he wrote *The Vanity of Human Wishes*. 'A man is never happy but when he is drunk,' he declared. Poor Johnson was drunk only once in his life, and his melancholy pervades every line of the poem:

> *'Enlarge my life with multitude of days,' –*
> *In health, in sickness, thus the suppliant prays,*
> *Hides from himself his state, and shuns to know*
> *That life protracted is protracted woe.*

Yet he finished on a note of hope: pray for 'obedient passions' (a significant phrase at this time), for a healthful mind, love, patience and faith:

> *With these celestial Wisdom calms the mind,*
> *And makes the happiness she does not find.*

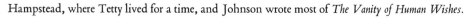

Hampstead, where Tetty lived for a time, and Johnson wrote most of *The Vanity of Human Wishes*.

Irene. Miss Wallis as Aspasia.

This calm, these joys, dear Innocence! are thine;
Joys ill exchangd for gold, and pride, and empire.

'When asked how he felt upon the ill success of his tragedy, he replied: "Like the Monument."' (*Boswell*)

Pleasure of life may be only the good hours of an ague, but at least there were good hours, and Johnson enjoyed them, for he had a great capacity for enjoyment when his melancholia lifted. In 1747 Garrick became manager of Drury Lane Theatre, and Johnson wrote him a prologue to speak at the opening. It is a brief history of the decline of English drama from Shakespeare's to Johnson's own day of 'Pantomime and Song'. But the audience gets the plays it deserves, so

'Tis yours, this night, to bid the reign commence
Of rescued Nature, and reviving Sense.

He was soon to have his chance to begin the new reign.

In 1749 Garrick produced *Irene* at Drury Lane. Johnson, whose normal dress was an old brown coat, now appeared in a box, resplendent in a scarlet waistcoat with rich gold lace, and a gold-laced hat. Before the curtain went up there were ominous catcalls and whistling, but the play went tolerably well until the final scene, when Irene was to be strangled on the stage. With the bowstring round her neck, she tried to speak her last lines, but the audience cried

'Irene'

'*Murder! Murder!*' and at length she had to leave the stage alive. The tragedy ran for nine nights, earning Johnson nearly £200, and Dodsley paid another £100 for the copyright. Yet it was not a success. What Johnson himself wrote about Addison's tragedy, *Cato*, applies with equal perfection to *Irene*: 'It is rather a poem in dialogue than a drama, rather a succession of just sentiments in elegant language, than a representation of natural affections.' There are memorable speeches:

> *Tomorrow's action! Can that hoary wisdom,*
> *Borne down with years, still doat upon tomorrow!*
> *That fatal mistress of the young, the lazy,*
> *The coward and the fool, condemn'd to lose*
> *An useless life in waiting for tomorrow,*
> *To gaze with longing eyes upon tomorrow,*
> *Till interposing death destroys the prospect.*
> *Strange! that this general fraud from day to day*
> *Should fill the world with wretches undetected.*
> *The soldier, lab'ring through a winter's march,*
> *Still sees tomorrow drest in robes of triumph;*
> *Still to the lover's long-expecting arms*
> *Tomorrow brings the visionary bride.*
> *But thou, too old to bear another cheat,*
> *Learn, that the present hour alone is man's.*

Although blank couplets rather than blank verse, and rhythmically monotonous, as spoken by Garrick the lines would be effective: but nobody could be interested in the part he played, the hero Demetrius, or in Irene, or any of the other characters.

Now that Tetty spent much of her time at Hampstead, Johnson spent much of his in conversation with friends, for 'there is in this world no real delight, excepting those of sensuality, but exchange of ideas in conversation,' and in 1749 he formed a club that met every Tuesday at the King's Head in Ivy Lane, near St Paul's. One of the nine members was his dearest friend, Richard Bathurst, a young physician and 'a very good hater', who shared Johnson's antipathy for fools, rogues and Whigs. Another was John Hawkins, a reserved and touchy attorney, 'a most unclubable man', who was to be Johnson's first biographer. With these companions he would sit late into the night, or early hours of the morning, drinking lemonade and talking, talking to postpone the hour of bed, solitude, loneliness and melancholy thoughts.

'*The Rambler*'   Although the Dictionary was not progressing as quickly as he had hoped, he embarked on another exacting venture, a series of essays to be published twice

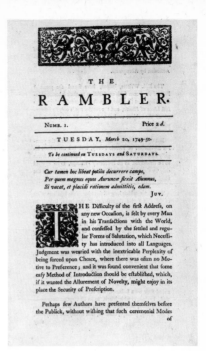

THE
RAMBLER.

NUMB. 1.   Price 2 d.

TUESDAY, March 20, 1749-50.

To be continued on TUESDAYS and SATURDAYS.

Cur tamen hoc libeat potius decurrere campo,
Per quem magnus equos Auruncæ flexit Alumnus,
Si vacat, et placidi rationem admittitis, edam.
                                        JUV.

THE Difficulty of the first Address, on any new Occasion, is felt by every Man in his Transactions with the World, and confessed by the settled and regular Forms of Salutation, which Necessity has introduced into all Languages. Judgment was wearied with the inextricable Perplexity of being forced upon Choice, where there was often no Motive to Preference; and it was found convenient that some easy Method of Introduction should be established, which, if it wanted the Allurement of Novelty, might enjoy in its place the Security of Prescription.

Perhaps few Authors have presented themselves before the Publick, without wishing that such ceremonial Modes of

'A most unclubable man.' Sir John Hawkins (1719–89) (*left*), Johnson's first biographer.

'I was at a loss how to name it . . . and resolved that I would not go to sleep till I had fixed its title.' (*right*)

a week, and called *The Rambler*. The first issue was on Tuesday, 20 March 1750, the last on Saturday, 14 March 1752, so that during these two years he wrote more than two hundred essays, many of them hurriedly, at the last moment. The essay has gone out of fashion, particularly the moralizing essay that might almost be a sermon, and so has the ponderous style of Johnson, with its latinisms and abstractions, its careful balance and antitheses. Yet his essays are by no means always sermons, nor is his prose always ponderous, but at its best approaches the sonority of Sir Thomas Browne's, which he so much admired:

> The proceedings of Time, though very dilatory, were, some few caprices excepted, conformable to justice: and many who thought themselves secure by a short forbearance, have sunk under his scythe, as they were posting down with their volumes in triumph to futurity.

Everywhere there is evidence of the man, devout, sincere, compassionate, who has reached his understanding of human nature through his own sufferings. His main object was to inculcate virtue, 'for it is always a writer's duty to make the world better'; but even in his own day readers were beginning to prefer moralizing made more palatable by fiction, Richardson's novels, *Pamela* and *Clarissa*, to the essays of *The Rambler*. 'I have never been much of a favourite with the public,' he wrote sadly in his last essay, yet his periodical was to bring him many friends and admirers, and it was consolatory to have Tetty say, 'I thought very well of you before; but I did not imagine you could have written anything equal to this.'

The widower   A few days after the publication of the last *Rambler*, Tetty died. Johnson was overcome with grief, and wrote to Taylor, who had recently been ordained, and was now in London: 'Let me have your company and instruction. Do not live away from me. My distress is great. . . . Remember me in your prayers, for vain is the help of man.' If there had been estrangement towards the end, it may well have added to his distress, and in the following March he wrote: 'I have kept this day as the anniversary of my Tetty's death, with prayer and tears.' He was thus to remember her for the last thirty years of his life.

Now that Tetty was gone, Johnson was even more lonely in the big house. He needed company and conversation at night, and if left alone would sometimes wander the streets and talk to prostitutes. For some years he had given bed and breakfast and an occasional Sunday dinner to Robert Levet, a physician who had picked up a knowledge of medicine in France, and practised among the poor of London, often accepting a drink instead of a fee.

'I laid this summer [1784] a stone over Tetty, in the chapel of Bromley, in Kent. The inscription is in Latin.'

Miss Anna Williams (1706–83) (*left*), the blind lady to whom Johnson gave refuge from 1752 till her death. Francis Barber (*c.* 1740–1801) (*right*), who entered Johnson's service in 1752, and was his principal legatee.

Johnson thought highly of his abilities, though he admitted that his appearance and behaviour disgusted the rich and terrified the poor. He now gave hospitality to a friend of Tetty's, Miss Anna Williams, recently blinded by cataract, an intelligent, well-educated woman and a good conversationalist, who presided over his tea-table and acted as housekeeper. Then, another new inmate arrived shortly after Tetty's death: Francis Barber, the negro servant of Dr Bathurst, who persuaded him to enter Johnson's service. Hawkins could never understand how Johnson employed him, for 'Diogenes himself never wanted a servant less than he seemed to do: the great bushy wig, which throughout his life he affected to wear . . . was ever nearly as impenetrable by a comb as a quickset hedge; and little of the dust that had once settled on his outer garments was ever known to have been disturbed by the brush.' However, Frank remained a lifelong faithful servant, though once he ran away to sea, an employment from which Johnson rescued him, for 'being in a ship is being in a jail, with the chance of being drowned.'

Thomas Warton (1728–90), Professor of Poetry, Oxford, and Poet Laureate.

'Seven years, my Lord, have now past since I waited in your outward rooms.' Johnson in the ante-room at Lord Chesterfield's. ▶

In the summer of 1754 Johnson visited Oxford for the first time since he had left it twenty-five years before, and was delighted to find that some of the servants of his old college remembered him. He was entertained by Thomas Warton, a future Professor of Poetry and Poet Laureate, and it was largely owing to him that the University honoured Johnson with a degree early in 1755. Meanwhile, Lord Chesterfield wrote two articles for a periodical in praise of Johnson and his Dictionary. He was supposed to be its patron, but had shown no interest in it since Johnson had addressed his *Plan* to him seven years before; now he was trying to make amends, in the hope that it would be dedicated to him. Johnson was not unnaturally angry at his thus trying to take credit for the work, and wrote a stinging letter:

Seven years, my Lord, have now past since I waited in your outward rooms, or was repulsed from your door; during which time I have been pushing on my work through difficulties of which it is useless to complain, and have brought it at last to the verge of publication, without one act of assistance, one word of encouragement, or one smile of favour. Such treatment I did not expect, for I never had a Patron before. . . .

Is not a Patron, my Lord, one who looks with unconcern on a man struggling for life in the water, and, when he has reached ground, encumbers him with help?

It was now that Johnson substituted *patron* for the original *garret* in the famous lines in *The Vanity of Human Wishes*:

> *Yet think what ills the scholar's life assail,*
> *Toil, envy, want, the patron and the jail.*

The last sheet of the Dictionary was taken to his publishers, and when the messenger returned, Johnson asked, 'Well, what did he say?' 'Sir,' answered the messenger, 'he said "Thank God I have done with him."' 'I am glad,' replied Johnson with a smile, 'that he thanks God for anything.' Then at last, after nearly nine years' labour, instead of the anticipated three, in April 1755 the two folio volumes appeared: *Dictionary of the English Language*, by Samuel Johnson, A.M.

'I knew that the work in which I engaged is generally considered as drudgery for the blind . . . beating the track of the alphabet with sluggish resolution.'

'His introducing his own opinions, and even prejudices . . . cannot be fully defended.' (*Boswell*) ▶

'Dictionary' Johnson   The Dictionary established Johnson's reputation. He was now 'Dictionary' Johnson, the Great Lexicographer, and he took his place in the front rank of men of letters. It was a great achievement, and did for the English language what he had set out to do: 'A dictionary by which the pronunciation of our language may be fixed, and its attainment facilitated; by which its purity may be preserved, its use ascertained, and its duration lengthened.' There were a few errors, and when a lady asked him why he defined *pastern* 'the *knee* of a horse', he replied, 'Ignorance, Madam, pure ignorance.' His definition of *network* was not very helpful: 'Anything reticulated or decussated, at equal distances, with interstices between the intersections.' Then, he allowed his prejudices to colour some of his definitions, *pension*, for example: 'An allowance made to anyone without an equivalent. In England it is generally understood to mean pay given to a state hireling for treason to his country.'

Garrick celebrated the publication with characteristic verses of gay nonsense:

> *Talk of war with a Briton, he'll boldly advance*
> *That one English soldier will beat ten of France . . .*
> *And Johnson, well arm'd like a hero of yore,*
> *Has beat forty French, and will beat forty more.*

EXCI′SE. *n. f.* [*accijs*, Dutch; *excisum*, Latin] A hateful tax levied upon commodities, and adjudged not by the common judges of property, but wretches hired by those to whom excise is paid.

The people should pay a ratable tax for their sheep, and an *excise* for every thing which they should eat.   *Hayward.*

          Ambitious now to take *excise*
Of a more fragrant paradise.   *Cleaveland.*
                              Excise,
With hundred rows of teeth, the shark exceeds,
And on all trades like Cassawar she feeds.   *Marvel.*
          Can hire large houses, and oppress the poor,
By farm'd *excise.*   *Dryden's Juvenal, Sat. 3.*

GRU′BSTREET. *n. f.* Originally the name of a street in Moorfields in London, much inhabited by writers of small histories, dictionaries, and temporary poems; whence any mean production is called *grubstreet.*

Χαῖρ Ἰθακὴ μετ᾽ ἄεθλα, μετ᾽ ἄλγεα πικρὰ
᾽Ασπασίως τέον ὖδας ἱκάνομαι.

The first part, though calculated only for the meridian of *grubstreet,* was yet taken notice of by the better sort. *Arbuthn.*
          I'd sooner ballads write, and *grubstreet* lays.   *Gay.*

LEXICO′GRAPHER. *n. f.* [λεξικὸν and γράφω; *lexicographe,* French.] A writer of dictionaries; a harmless drudge, that busies himself in tracing the original, and detailing the signification of words.

Commentators and *lexicographers* acquainted with the Syriac language, have given these hints in their writings on scripture.   *Watts's Improvement of the Mind.*

OATS. *n. f.* [aten, Saxon.] A grain, which in England is generally given to horses, but in Scotland supports the people.

FOUR NEW FRIENDS: Joshua Reynolds (1723–92) (*left*), knighted 1769. 'Sir Joshua Reynolds possesses the largest share of inoffensiveness of any man that I know.' Miss Frances Reynolds (*right*), Sir Joshua's sister (1729–1807). 'Her mind . . . is very near to purity itself.'

Johnson, however, was in no mood of gaiety. After the immense labour came the reaction, and he finished his preface on a note of despondency:

I may surely be contented without the praise of perfection, which, if I could obtain in this gloom of solitude, what would it avail me? I have protracted my work till most of those whom I wished to please have sunk into the grave; and success and miscarriage are empty sounds. I therefore dismiss it with frigid tranquillity, having little to fear or hope from censure or from praise.

He was thinking mainly of Tetty, but others too had gone, among them Cave, one of whose last acts had been fondly to press his hand, and some of the members of the Ivy Lane Club, which now broke up. But 'A man,' he said, 'should keep his friendship in constant repair,' and he was already enriching his life with new and valued friends.

New friends   First among these was Joshua Reynolds, who in 1752 returned from Italy, partially deafened by a severe cold that he caught there, and, though only twenty-nine, quickly established himself as a fashionable portrait painter. *The Life of Richard Savage*, read in absorption while standing up, first roused his interest in Johnson, and when they met soon afterwards they became firm friends. Johnson also thought very highly of Miss Reynolds, the painter's sister, whose mind was 'very near to purity itself'.

Bennet Langton (1737–1801)
'The earth does not bear a worthier man.'

Topham Beauclerk (1738–80)
'Such another will not easily be found
among mankind.'

He liked young men, partly because they best kept friendship in repair, partly because 'a man commonly grows wickeder as he grows older'. There was Bennet Langton, of an old Lincolnshire family, a tall, slender young man, resembling a stork standing on one leg, and appropriately known as Lanky. Amiable, gentle, a fine scholar, and an admirer of *The Rambler*, he secured an invitation to Gough Square, where he expected to meet a decorous philosopher; 'Instead of which, down from his bedchamber, about noon, came, as newly risen, a huge uncouth figure with a little dark wig which scarcely covered his head, and his clothes hanging loose about him.' Langton was so impressed by his conversation that he came to revere him as a father, and Johnson loved the young man as a son. 'I know not who will go to heaven if Langton does not,' he said.

First, however, Langton went to Oxford, where he introduced Johnson to his fellow-undergraduate Topham Beauclerk, an elegant Restoration rake born a century too late. He was indeed a descendant of Charles II, whom he resembled; but he was also a great lover of literature and a brilliant talker. 'No man,' said Johnson, 'ever was so free, when he was going to say a good thing, from a look that expressed that it was coming; or, when he had said it, from a look that expressed that it had come.'

One night, Beau and Lanky, having sat in a London tavern till three in the morning, decided to call up Johnson. He appeared in his shirt, a little black wig on top of his head, and a poker in his hand. When they asked him to join them, he cried, 'What, is it you, you dogs! I'll have a frisk with you!' So Johnson and his two young friends, thirty years younger than himself, brewed a bowl of bishop in a tavern, rambled through Covent Garden, and rowed a boat to Billingsgate, where Langton left the other two to continue their dissipation. When Garrick heard the story, he told Johnson that his frolic would get him into the newspapers. '*He* durst not do such a thing,' Johnson said later 'his *wife* would not *let* him.'

'The man who is tired of London is tired of life.' Covent Garden (*above*). Billingsgate (*above right*) 'Fleet Street has a very animated appearance (*below left*); but I think the full tide of human existence is at Charing Cross (*below right*).'

Although Johnson was now the Great Cham of literature, as Smollett called him, he was still very poor. He had spent on the Dictionary all the money that had been advanced, and continued to help his assistants; having no capital, he still had to 'provide for the day that was passing over him', and in March 1756 was 'under an arrest for five pounds eighteen shillings', until rescued by a loan from Richardson. Langton's father offered him a living in Lincolnshire if he chose to be ordained, but he refused. The regular duties of a parson were not for him, still less those of a country parson for a man who had come to love London as he did. 'The man who is tired of London,' he said, 'is tired of life.' So he wrote for another periodical *The Literary Magazine*, and issued *Proposals for a New Edition of Shakespear*. 'The corruptions of the text,' he wrote, 'will be corrected by a careful collation of all the oldest copies,' and he promised subscribers that the work would be published before Christmas 1757. At Christmas 1757 he wrote, 'I shall publish about March,' but it was to be another eight years before his *Shakespear* appeared.

'The Idler'   Meanwhile, from April 1758 to April 1760 he wrote another series of essays, called *The Idler*, for a weekly periodical. Johnson himself is the Idler, of course, as in the former series he was the Rambler, and in Number 31 he comes near to a self-portrait in the character of Sober:

> Sober is a man of strong desires and quick imagination, so exactly balanced by the love of ease, that they can seldom stimulate him to any difficult under-taking. . . .
> Mr Sober's chief pleasure is conversation: there is no end of his talk or his attention. . . . But there is one time at night when he must go home, that his friends may sleep; and another time in the morning, when all the world agrees to shut out interruption. These are the moments of which poor Sober trembles at the thought. But the misery of these tiresome intervals he has many means of alleviating. . . . He has a small furnace, which he employs in distillation, and which has long been the solace of his life.

Soon after he had written this essay, Lucy Porter wrote from Lichfield to tell him that his mother, 'Granny', as she called her, now aged ninety, was seriously ill. He had not seen her for nearly twenty years, since his last visit in 1739–40. He wrote a number of comforting letters, sent money, and prepared to go to Lichfield, an expensive journey that took twenty-six hours; but she died in January 1759, and in Number 41 of *The Idler*, 'On the Death of a Friend', he expressed his grief and desolation.

'Rasselas'   The middle of the eighteenth century was the period of the rise and rapid development of the novel. Richardson's *Pamela* and *Clarissa*, Fielding's *Joseph Andrews* and *Tom Jones* had appeared in the 1740s, and by 1759 Sterne's

Johnson in 1756. 'I found that I had a very perfect idea of Johnson's figure, from the portrait ▶ painted of him by Sir Joshua Reynolds . . . sitting in his easy chair in deep meditation.' (*Boswell*)

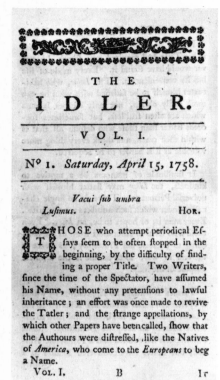

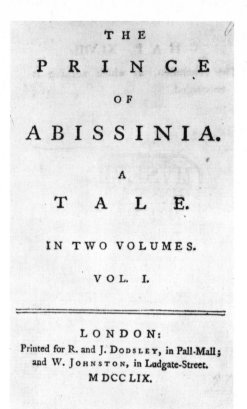

Tristram Shandy was in the press. Johnson had no use for Fielding, an immoral 'barren rascal'; his friend Richardson was the man, though he admitted, 'if you were to read Richardson for the story, your impatience would be so much fretted that you would hang yourself. You must read him for the sentiment.' So Johnson decided to write a novel for the sentiment, and with the proceeds pay for his mother's funeral. He wrote it in the evenings of a single week, and by the end of March *Rasselas* was on sale.

Ye who listen with credulity to the whispers of fancy, and pursue with eagerness the phantoms of hope; who expect that age will perform the promises of youth, and that the deficiencies of the present day will be supplied by the morrow; attend to the history of Rasselas, Prince of Abyssinia.

Such is the opening paragraph of *Rasselas*, a novel, or moral fable, consisting mainly of conversations led by Johnson himself in the person of the philosophic Imlac; for the book is a moving prose version of *The Vanity of Human Wishes*, the hopeless quest of man for happiness.

THREE CONTEMPORARY
NOVELISTS:

Henry Fielding (1707–54). 'What I
mean by his being a blockhead is,
that he was a barren rascal.'

Laurence Sterne (1713–68).
'Nothing odd will do long. *Tristram
Shandy* did not last.'

Samuel Richardson (1689–1761).
'There is more knowledge of the
heart in one letter of Richardson's
than in all *Tom Jones*.'

53

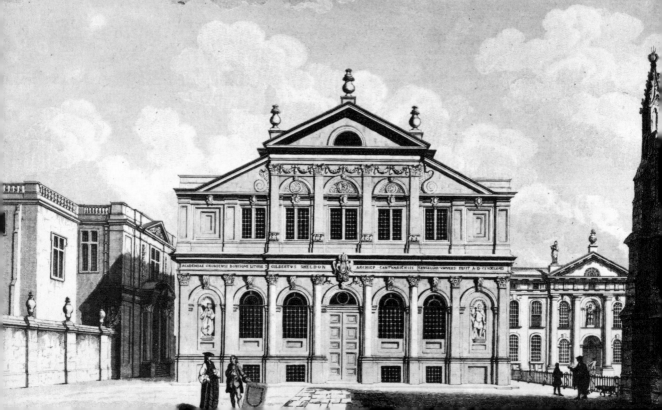

A view from the north, and
(*below*) Wren's Sheldonian Theatre.
'I have been in my gown ever
since I came here,' wrote
Johnson in 1759.

'He removed to chambers in the
Inner Temple Lane, where he
lived in poverty, total idleness,
and the pride of literature'.
(*Arthur Murphy*)
Johnson's rooms, 1760–65, were
on the first floor, above the lamp.
It was here that Murphy brought
him the news of his pension.

There were, however, intervals of happiness, and when Johnson went to
Oxford at midsummer, he took to swimming again, drank three bottles of port
at a sitting, and challenged a companion to climb the college wall. He wore his
new MA gown on all occasions, and joined the procession to the Sheldonian
Theatre for the election of the Chancellor of the University.

A visit to Lichfield in the following winter was less exhilarating. Few people
knew him; his former playfellows were elderly men, reminding him that he was
now fifty-two, and Lucy Porter had lost her youth and gaiety, without gaining
wisdom. He wandered about for five days, and then returned to London, to
chambers in the Inner Temple.

'We were so weary of our old king, that we are much pleased with his successor.'
George III, whose accession in 1760, when only twenty-two, led to a new phase in Johnson's life.

A pension   The accession of George III in 1760 was to revolutionize Johnson's life, for in 1762 the young King offered him a pension of £300 a year, a sum sufficient to maintain him in comfort for life. He was in a difficult position: he was a professed Jacobite, and in his Dictionary had defined *pension* as 'pay given to a state hireling for treason to his country'. He consulted Reynolds, who assured him that the definition did not apply to him, and when the Prime Minister, Lord Bute, told him, 'It is not given you for anything you are to do, but for what you have done', he accepted. 'I hope you will now purge, and live cleanly like a gentleman,' said Beauclerk, adapting the words of Falstaff.

His acceptance lost him the companionship of Thomas Sheridan, a former actor and teacher of elocution. When Johnson heard that he too had been given a pension, he exclaimed, 'What! have they given *him* a pension? Then it is time for me to give up mine.' Sheridan heard of it, though not Johnson's addition: 'However, I am glad that Mr Sheridan has a pension, for he is a very good man.' Sheridan refused to be reconciled, and never spoke to Johnson again.

At the age of fifty-three, with only a blind woman to look after him, Johnson cannot have been a pretty sight. A big, strong, clumsy man, he never enjoyed good health; his face was disfigured by scars, his walk that of a man in fetters, and when he sat, his head, inclined to the right, shook tremulously as his body swayed backwards and forwards, while he clucked and muttered and whistled, before blowing out his breath like a whale. In the street his convulsive movements were even more remarkable; sometimes he would stop and whirl about, or imitate the action of a galloping jockey, and he would stride across a threshold as if to see how far he could reach. He was a gross feeder, but for most of his later life did not drink wine; he could abstain, but could not be temperate, and he drank prodigious quantities of tea, with which he cheered himself in the morning, and solaced himself in the evening. His dress was slovenly rather than eccentric: dark and dingy coat and breeches, black stockings and grubby linen, his wig singed at the front by the candle-flame he read by.

Johnson's description of *Tea*.

TEA. *n. ſ.* [a word, I ſuppoſe, Chineſe; *thé*, Fr.] A Chineſe plant, of which the infuſion has lately been much drunk in Europe.

> The muſes friend, *tea*, does our fancy aid,
> Repreſs thoſe vapours which the head invade.   *Waller.*
> One has a deſign of keeping an open *tea* table.   *Addiſon.*
> I have filled a *tea* pot, and received a diſh of it.   *Addiſon.*
> He ſwept down a dozen *tea* diſhes.   *Spectator.*
> Nor will you encourage the common *tea* table talk. *Spect.*
> Green leaves of *tea* contain a narcotick juice, which exudes by roaſting: this is performed with great care before it is expoſed to ſale.   *Arbuthnot on Aliments.*
> Here living *tea* pot ſtands; one arm held out,
> One bent; the handle this, and that the ſpout.   *Pope.*
> The miſtreſs of the *tea* ſhop may give half an ounce. *Sw.*
> The fear of being thought pedants hath taken many young divines off from their ſeverer ſtudies, which they have exchanged for plays, in order to qualify them for *tea* tables.   *Swift.*
> When you ſweep, never ſtay to pick up *tea* ſpoons. *Swift.*

The big tremulous head of this uncouth giant housed one of the most power-ful minds of the age, yet a mind always in conflict. Religion was his solace, and he clung desperately to the dogma of the Church of England, for it offered him happiness after the 'protracted woe' of this life; but there was a whiff of brim-stone, too, and his own high standard of conduct, his very virtues, made him fear damnation. No wonder the man thus torn between hope and fear savagely attacked those who tried to shake his faith, and was easily moved to anger. His more general irritability and aggressiveness, however, were probably defensive in origin; he was a man of humble birth, who had suffered poverty, privation, neglect and humiliation, yet by his courage, tenacity and exertions had at last achieved recognition and fame, and it was now his turn to dominate and demonstrate the superiority of his genius.

Yet, as Goldsmith said, he had 'nothing of the bear but his skin'. Although he could be harsh and rude, he was essentially gentle and considerate, and if he spoke too roughly in the heat of the moment, he would generally apologize. He even considered himself a polite man, particularly to ladies, whom he could charm with flattery, and captivate with his attentions. Honest and truthful, he detested cant, humbug and affectation, and his earthy common sense demolished the airy erections of credulity. Humane and benevolent, he disapproved of slavery, but believed in rank and a due subordination, and he was perverse in his prejudice against Whigs, Scots and Americans. Nature and the visual arts meant little to him, for he could scarcely see them, and music was merely a noise indistinctly heard.

He was at his happiest and best in conversation and argument, for then the exhilaration of talking for victory made him forget his melancholy, and he would laugh, a good-humoured growl, or, as Tom Davies described it, 'like a rhinoceros'. His voice was loud, his speech slow and deliberate, his argument logical and illuminated by imagery, and all the more impressive, perhaps, for the rich provincialisms: *there* rhymed with *fear*, *once* was *woonse*, and Garrick would imitate him, squeezing a lemon into a punch-bowl with uncouth gesticulations, looking round the company, and calling, 'Who's for poonsh?'

This was the formidable figure that entered Tom Davies's bookshop in Russell Street, Covent Garden, on that memorable evening of 16 May 1763.

Enter Boswell It was seven o'clock, and Mr and Mrs Davies were entertaining a visitor to tea. The visitor was James Boswell, a diminutive Scot, aged twenty-two, who had come to London in search of a commission in the Guards. His father, however, Lord Auchinleck, a judge, had different ideas, and insisted on his heir becom-ing a lawyer. Boswell had just agreed to study law if he could go abroad to do so, and in the meantime was pursuing his amorous adventures in London, and

Tom Davies's bookshop, 8 Russell Street, where Boswell first met Johnson. 'On Monday the 16th of May, when I was sitting in Mr Davies's back-parlour . . . Johnson unexpectedly came into the shop.' ▶

Tom Davies (1712–85), actor, dramatist and bookseller. 'Though somewhat pompous, he was an entertaining companion . . . a friendly and very hospitable man.' (*Boswell*)

'Give me your hand; I have taken a liking to you.' James Boswell in 1765, aged twenty-five. ▶

stalking the eminent Rambler, whom he was just about to encounter. The meeting must be described in Boswell's own words, an elaboration of his entry in his journal.

Mr Davies mentioned my name, and respectfully introduced me to him. I was much agitated; and recollecting his prejudice against the Scotch, of which I had heard much, I said to Davies, 'Don't tell where I come from.' 'From Scotland,' cried Davies roguishly. 'Mr Johnson, (said I) I do indeed come from Scotland, but I cannot help it.' I am willing to flatter myself that I meant this as a light pleasantry to soothe and conciliate him, and not as an humiliating abasement at the expense of my country. But however that might be, this speech was somewhat unlucky; for with that quickness of wit for which he was so remarkable, he seized the expression 'come from Scotland', which I used in the sense of being of that country; and, as if I had said that I had come away from it, or left it, retorted, 'That, Sir, I find, is what a very great many of your countrymen cannot help.' This stroke stunned me a good deal; and when we had sat down, I felt myself not a little embarrassed, and apprehensive of what might come next. He then addressed himself to Davies: 'What do you think of Garrick? He has refused me an order for the

Temple Bar, Fleet Street. 'I remember once being with Goldsmith in Westminster Abbey. While we surveyed the Poets' Corner, I said to him: "*Forsitan et nostrum nomen miscebitur istis.*" [Perhaps our name will be mingled with these.] When we got to Temple Bar, he stopped me, pointed to the heads [of criminals] upon it, and slily whispered me: "*Forsitan et nostrum nomen miscebitur ISTIS!*"'.

play for Miss Williams, because he knows the house will be full, and that an order will be worth three shillings.' Eager to take any opening to get into conversation with him, I ventured to say, 'O, Sir, I cannot think Mr Garrick would grudge such a trifle to you.' 'Sir, (said he, with a stern look) I have known David Garrick longer than you have done: and I know no right you have to talk to me on the subject.'

After two such knockdown blows, anyone less resilient than Boswell would have crept away, but he stayed on, fascinated by the extraordinary vigour of Johnson's conversation; and when he left, he was consoled when Davies whispered, 'Don't be uneasy. I can see he likes you very well.'

A week later he called on Johnson, and was astonished at the disorder of his room and dress. Johnson, loath to let an amiable young hero-worshipper go, pressed him time and again to stay, and even promised to return his visit. 'I generally go abroad at four in the afternoon,' he informed him, 'and seldom come home till two in the morning.' A few days later they met near Temple Bar at one o'clock in the morning. That was probably the night on which Boswell had his pocket picked by a prostitute whom he took 'into Privy Garden and indulged sensuality'.

On 25 June Boswell got Johnson to himself for a whole evening, when they supped at the Mitre Tavern in Fleet Street. Johnson talked about Gray, 'not a first-rate poet. He has not a bold imagination, nor much command of

'My next meeting with Johnson was on Friday the 1st of July (1763), when he and I and Dr Goldsmith supped at the Mitre.... Goldsmith's respectful attachment to Johnson was then at its height; for his own literary reputation had not yet distinguished him so much as to excite a vain desire of competition with his great Master.' (*Boswell*)

words.' He talked about ghosts, in which he was inclined to believe, and about Goldsmith, 'one of the first men we now have as an author'. Then Boswell introduced the subject of the evening: Boswell. A rudderless young man in search of a sympathetic father, he gave Johnson a sketch of his life, presumably bowdlerized, for the Moralist took his hand and protested, 'I have taken a liking to you,' and promised to give him a plan of study and conduct.

There was another supper at the Mitre, this time with a third member of the party, Oliver Goldsmith, an improvident Irish genius of thirty-five, who had just won recognition with his *Chinese Letters*. Johnson had known him for about two years, and was soon to save him from a debtors' prison by sending him a guinea, and arranging the sale of his *Vicar of Wakefield* for £60. Tonight, when the party broke up, Goldsmith strutted away with Johnson, calling proudly to Boswell, 'I go to Miss Williams.' To drink tea with Miss Williams, now in lodgings near the Temple, was the final proof of intimacy with Johnson, who drank tea with her every night, however late. Boswell envied Goldsmith, but it was not long before he too went to Miss Williams.

The friendship between Johnson and Boswell ripened rapidly. There were more suppers at the Mitre, and at the Turk's Head in the Strand, and an expedition down the Thames to Greenwich. 'We walked in the evening in Greenwich Park,' wrote Boswell.

Greenwich Hospital, designed by Wren. 'He remarked that the structure . . . was too magnificent for a place of charity, and that its parts were too much detached to make one great whole.'

Oliver Goldsmith (1728–74). 'He was not an agreeable companion, for he talked always for fame. A man who does so, never can be pleasing.'

He asked me, I suppose by way of trying my disposition, 'Is not this very fine?' Having no exquisite relish of the beauties of Nature, and being more delighted with 'the busy hum of men', I answered, 'Yes, Sir, but not equal to Fleet Street.' JOHNSON. 'You are right, Sir.'

Then, a proof of friendship indeed, Johnson proposed seeing his young friend 'out of England'. On 5 August the two set out in the Harwich stage-coach, and on the 7th Boswell embarked for Holland, to study law at Utrecht. It was to be February 1766 before he returned, after a happy thirty months in pursuit of women and famous men. The persistent, adhesive young Scot failed to get an interview with Frederick the Great of Prussia, but he bagged Rousseau,

Edmund Burke (1729–97). 'That fellow calls forth all my powers; were I to see Burke now, it would kill me.'

A literary party at Sir Joshua Reynolds's house: Boswell, Johnson, Reynolds, Garrick, Burke, Paoli, Burney, Warton, Goldsmith.

Voltaire and General Paoli, the heroic leader of the Corsican revolt against Genoese dominion.

Soon after Boswell's departure, Reynolds and Johnson formed the famous Literary Club, among the other original nine members being Goldsmith, Hawkins, Beauclerk, Langton and Edmund Burke, another young Irishman for whom Johnson had the greatest admiration: 'an extraordinary man, his stream of mind is perpetual'. When Reynolds mentioned the Club to Garrick, 'I like it much,' he said, 'I think I shall be of you.' Johnson was furious: '*He'll be of us!* How does he know we'll permit him? The first duke in England has no right to use such language.' However, he was eventually elected – ten years later.

The Literary Club

Charles Churchill (1731–64). 'His poetry had a temporary currency, only from its audacity of abuse, and being filled with living names. . . . I called the fellow a blockhead at first, and I will call him a blockhead still.'

Now that Johnson had a steady income, he could afford to travel. In 1762 he went with Reynolds, a Devonshireman, to Plymouth; in 1764 he stayed with the Langtons in Lincolnshire and with Dr Percy in Northamptonshire, and in 1765 paid a short visit to Cambridge.

It was now nine years since he had issued his proposals for a new edition of Shakespeare, and promised subscribers that it would be published by the end of 1757. He should have been collating all the oldest copies he could find, again as he had promised subscribers; but the years went by, until in 1762 Charles Churchill, a dissolute parson and able satirist, attacked him as Pomposo in *The Ghost*:

> *Pomposo, insolent and loud,*
> *Vain idol of a scribbling crowd,*
> *Whose very name inspires an awe,*
> *Whose every word is sense and law, . . .*
> *Horrid, unwieldy, without form,*
> *Savage as ocean in a storm, . . .*
> *He for subscribers baits his hook,*
> *And takes their cash — but where's the book?*
> *No matter where — wise fear, we know,*
> *Forbids the robbing of a foe;*
> *But what, to serve our private ends,*
> *Forbids the cheating of our friends?*

Johnson may have been stung into belated, though intermittent, action, and the eight volumes of his edition appeared in 1765.

Johnson lacked the industry and patience essential to a good editor, and he contributed little to the elucidation of Shakespeare's text. His *Preface*, however, is one of the best things he wrote. Although he seemed almost unaware that Shakespeare was a poet, he defended him against the attacks of pedantry, and rescued him from the excesses of adulation, summing up judicially the faults as well as the virtues of his plays, as he saw them. Shortly after the publication, Trinity College, Dublin, awarded him the degree of Doctor of Laws.

Edition of Shakespeare

'Early in 1764 Johnson paid a visit to the Langton family, at their seat of Langton in Lincolnshire, where he passed some time, much to his satisfaction.' (*Boswell*) It was here that, having walked up a hill, he insisted on rolling down.

The beginning of sixteen years of luxury for Johnson. Henry and Hester Thrale, and their daughter 'Queeney'. 'She is more flippant: he is a regular scholar; but her learning is that of a schoolboy in one of the lower forms.'

Henry and Hester Thrale It was in this year, 1765, that Arthur Murphy, an Irish actor and dramatist, introduced Johnson to Mr and Mrs Thrale, a young couple who by their friendship were again to revolutionize his life. Henry Thrale was a large, lethargic man of thirty-seven, a wealthy brewer, a Member of Parliament, and a prodigious eater. He had a town-house near the brewery in his Southwark constituency, a country-house at Streatham, six miles away, and a third at Brighton. His wife Hester, only twenty-four, was a small, vivacious, intelligent woman, who offered Johnson the care, comforts and affection he so much needed. Her 'master', as she called her husband, was very much the master, and probably the only man who could silence Johnson. 'There, there,' he would say, 'Now we have had enough for one lecture. We will not be upon education any more till after dinner, if you please.' And at the parlour door his valet would give Johnson a fresh wig to replace the singed one he was wearing.

In spite of his taciturnity, Thrale was devoted to good conversation, while Hester's ambition was to be mistress of a *salon*. Their marriage, in 1763, had been one of convenience, not love, but they agreed that Johnson, the best talker

Streatham Place. 'I long to come to that place which my dear friends allow me to call *home*.' ▶

(*above*) 'Our journey to Streatham was the least pleasant part of the day, for the roads were dreadfully dusty.' (*Fanny Burney*) A view of the hill near Five Mile Stone, on the road to Streatham.

The summer-house at Streatham (*far right*). 'Soon after Dr Johnson went, I went, and shut myself up in a sweet cool summer-house, to read *Irene*.' (*Fanny Burney*)

Johnson's Court, Fleet Street. When not with the Thrales, Johnson lived here from 1765 to 1776. Boswell had 'a veneration for this court'. ▶

and leading literary lion of his age, would be an invaluable asset, who with his friends, such men as Reynolds, Goldsmith, Garrick, Burney and Burke, would make Streatham Place one of the cultural centres of England. A room was assigned to him, the library restocked, and he was told to make their house his home whenever he wished. 'No man but a blockhead ever wrote except for money,' he maintained, and now that he was provided with board and lodging, and had all luxuries paid for, he wrote nothing of importance for the next ten years, spending most of his time with the Thrales, either at the Brewery House, or in the summer at Streatham Place.

This suited Boswell, for now that he was about to become an Edinburgh lawyer, his London jaunts were confined to the law vacations in spring and autumn. When he returned to England in February 1766, therefore, he found Johnson in London, in a house in Johnson's Court, Fleet Street, with Miss Williams on the ground floor, Levet in the garret, and Frank in attendance.

'The Queen's House',
now Buckingham Palace, in the library of which
Johnson met the young king George III in 1767.

There were more suppers at the Mitre, though Johnson now drank only water or lemonade. He was continually making good resolutions, which he rarely kept, though for some time after New Year's Day he rose at eight instead of the customary noon. In this year he was sick both in body and mind, but the country air of Streatham did him good, as did the devoted attentions of Mrs Thrale, who would sit up with him, talking and making tea until the early hours of the morning.

In the following February occurred an event that Johnson delighted to relate to his friends. One day, while reading in the royal library at the Queen's House, the King came into the room. As was his way, he asked a number of questions,

'His Majesty having the preceding year [1768] instituted the Royal Academy of Arts in London, Johnson had now the honour of being appointed Professor in Ancient Literature.' (*Boswell*) The Exhibition of 1771.

among them: Was he then writing anything? Johnson replied that he thought he had done his part as a writer. 'I should have thought so too,' said the King, 'if you had not written so well.' When asked if he made any reply to this high compliment, Johnson answered, 'No, Sir. When the King had said it, it was to be so. It was not for me to bandy civilities with my Sovereign. . . . Sir, they may talk of the King as they will; but he is the finest gentleman I have ever seen.' It reminds one of the story of Oscar Browning, the Cambridge don, who was once presented to the Kaiser: 'One of the nicest Emperors I have ever met.' But there was nothing snobbish about Johnson, and the story merely illustrates his reverence for the monarchy as the symbol of a settled order.

He was always ready to help those in need. 'He gave away all he had,' wrote Mrs Thrale. 'All he did was gentle, if all he said was rough.' He would put pennies in the hands of children sleeping in the streets, and while staying at Streatham returned every weekend to give his dependants three good dinners. Although far from well at this time, the late 1760s, he helped Miss Williams to publish a volume of verse, wrote a prologue for Goldsmith's comedy, *The Good-Natured Man*, and in 1769 was largely responsible for clearing the Italian writer Joseph Baretti of a charge of murder. He did not go to Stratford, however, to support Garrick, who organized a Shakespeare Jubilee in the town. Perhaps he knew it would be mainly a Garrick Jubilee, and he preferred to go with the Thrales to Brighton, even though he disliked the bare chalk downs. But Boswell attended the junketings. He had just published – and reviewed – his *Account of Corsica*, and appeared appropriately as a Corsican patriot.

The Shakespeare Jubilee at Stratford, September 1769. Garrick recites:

Untouch'd and sacred be thy shrine,
Avonian Willy, bard divine,
In studious posture leaning! ▶

'Corsica' Boswell (*below right*) attends the Jubilee, but Johnson writes from Brighton (*below*): 'I do not find that I am likely to come back very soon from this place.'

After the Jubilee, Johnson and Boswell met frequently in London. On 6 October Boswell paid his first visit to Streatham, on the 10th he introduced Johnson to the exiled Paoli, and on the 16th gave a dinner-party at his lodgings in Old Bond Street. His guests were Reynolds, Garrick, Goldsmith, Tom Davies, Arthur Murphy, and of course Johnson. 'Garrick played round him with a fond vivacity, taking hold of the breasts of his coat, and, looking up in his face with a lively archness, complimented him on the good health which he seemed then to enjoy; while the sage, shaking his head, beheld him with a gentle complacency.' One of the guests was late, and Boswell asked if six people should be kept waiting for one. 'Why, yes,' answered Johnson, 'if the one will suffer more by your sitting down, than the six will do by waiting.' The talk turned naturally on Shakespeare, Johnson contending that the description of the temple in Congreve's *Mourning Bride* was finer than any descriptive passage in Shakespeare. On the 19th Boswell passed the evening with Johnson at his house, when they talked of our feeling for the distresses of others. 'Why, Sir, there is much noise made about it, but it is greatly exaggerated. . . . Why, there's Baretti, who is to be tried for his life tomorrow; friends have risen up for him on every side, yet if he should be hanged, none of them will eat a slice of plum-pudding the less.' On the 26th they dined together at the Mitre, then went to tea with Miss Williams, where there was 'a pretty large circle'. Johnson talked for victory: 'No, Sir, medicated baths can be no better than warm water: their only effect can be that of tepid moisture.' When one of the company protested, Johnson turned on him with, 'Well, Sir, go and get thyself fumi-gated; but be sure that the steam be directed to thy *head*, for *that* is the peccant part.' 'There is no arguing with Johnson,' said Goldsmith, 'for when his pistol misses fire, he knocks you down with the butt end of it.'

Johnson rarely started a subject: 'You are like a ghost,' Tom Tyers once remarked, 'you will never speak till you are spoken to.' It was Boswell's business to find a theme, and he now asked, 'If, Sir, you were shut up in a castle, and a new-born child with you, what would you do?' It was not a very successful opening, so Boswell tried again, and introduced the subject of death. It was the subject that Johnson always tried to forget, and Boswell's persevering prods threw him into such a passion that he said things that even Boswell did not care to record, told him to go away, and shouted, 'Don't let us meet tomorrow.' When Boswell called on the following morning, Johnson was in good humour and on 10 November he came from Streatham to see him off for Scotland to be married. He did not return until March 1772.

By then Johnson was in better health and spirits, thanks largely to the attentions of Mrs Thrale: 'Ready to become a scoundrel, Madam; with a little more spoiling you will, I think, make me a complete rascal.' Her husband loved

Joseph Baretti (*above left*). One of the portraits painted by Reynolds for the Thrale library at ▶
Streatham, where he was for a time Italian tutor.
'General Paoli (*below left*) has the loftiest port of any man I have ever seen.'

Johnson (*above*) writes to Mrs Thrale before setting off for Lichfield. 20 June 1771.

food as much as did Johnson, whose favourite Streatham dishes were a leg of pork boiled till it dropped from the bone, a veal pie with plums and sugar, and the outside cut of a salt buttock of beef. He liked plenty of cream or melted butter in his chocolate, and was so fond of fruit that he ate seven or eight large peaches before breakfast. Such luxury did not encourage literary labour, and the pattern of his life in the 1770s, a relatively happy decade devoted mainly to talking, was much the same each year: Streatham for seven or eight months, a weekly dinner at the Club, and in the autumn a jaunt to Lichfield, Ashbourne, Birmingham and Oxford, There were to be longer excursions in 1773 and the two following years.

'Sir, I am a great friend to public amusements, for they keep people from vice.'

A Chop House (*left*) and Coffee House (*below*) in the early 1780s.

(*above right*) Johnson, Boswell, Mrs Thrale and Goldsmith in a supper-box at Vauxhall Gardens.

(*below right*) 'We then walked to the Pantheon.' (*Boswell*, ▶ 31 March 1772.) The Pantheon, Oxford Street, designed by James Wyatt as a centre for masquerades, had just been finished.

80

One of the City churches rebuilt by Wren after the Great Fire of 1666: St Clement Danes, Strand, 'where he had his seat; and his behaviour was solemnly devout'. (*Boswell*, Good Friday, 1773)

In 1773 Boswell arrived in London shortly before Easter, and on Good Friday accompanied Johnson to his favourite church, St Clement Danes. They had breakfasted on cross-buns and tea (without milk) made by Levet, and to Boswell's surprise Johnson asked him to dine on Easter Day. He had never heard of anybody being invited to dinner, but Johnson explained that on Sundays he generally had a meat pie, boiled at a public oven: a very proper arrangement, as it enabled servants to go to church. Boswell half expected to have to eat some outlandish dish with his fingers, but found all in good order, with Miss Williams as hostess, and was able to tell inquisitive friends that they had a very good soup, a boiled leg of lamb and spinach, and rice-pudding.

To SAMUEL JOHNSON, L.L D.

Dear Sir,

BY inscribing this slight performance to you, I do not mean so much to compliment you as myself. It may do me some honour to inform the public, that I have lived many years in intimacy with you. It may serve the interests of mankind also to inform them, that the greatest wit may be found in a character, without impairing the most unaffected piety.

I have, particularly, reason to thank you for your partiality to this performance. The undertaking a comedy, not merely sentimental, was very dangerous; and Mr. Colman, who saw this piece in its various stages, always thought it so. However I ventured to trust it to the public; and though it was necessarily delayed till late in the season, I have every reason to be grateful.

I am, Dear Sir,

Your most sincere friend,

And admirer,

OLIVER GOLDSMITH.

A fortnight later Boswell dined at Beauclerk's with Johnson, Reynolds and some other members of the Club. Goldsmith being mentioned, Johnson said, 'It is amazing how little Goldsmith knows. He seldom comes where he is not more ignorant than anyone else.' 'Yet,' said Reynolds, 'there is no man whose company is more liked.' 'To be sure, Sir,' Johnson continued, 'when people find a man of the most distinguished abilities as a writer, their inferior while he is with them, it must be highly gratifying to them. What Goldsmith comically says of himself is very true – he always gets the better when he argues alone; meaning that he is master of a subject in his study, and can write well upon it; but when he comes into company, grows confused, and unable to talk. . . . Whether, indeed, we take him as a poet, as a comic writer, or as an historian, he stands in the first class.'

It was an important occasion for Boswell, as after dinner he was to be balloted for as a member of the Club. He was duly elected, and introduced to its distinguished members, among them Burke, whom he now met for the first time. Johnson, leaning on a chair as on a pulpit, with humorous formality explained the conduct expected of him as a good member of the Club.

For many years Boswell had urged Johnson to visit Scotland and the Hebrides, and at last he had agreed to make the journey. On his return to Edinburgh, therefore, Boswell wrote, pressing him to keep his promise, and two months later Johnson replied: 'I hope your dear lady and her dear baby are both well. I shall see them too when I come; and I have that opinion of your choice, as to suspect that when I have seen Mrs Boswell, I shall be less willing to go away.'

Mrs James Boswell (*c.* 1738–89). She was Margaret Montgomerie, Boswell's cousin.

'Scotland is little known to the ▶ greater part of those who may read these observations.'

Edinburgh Castle.

'Old Aberdeen is the ancient episcopal city, in which are still to be seen the remains of the cathedral.'

To Scotland with Boswell On 14 August Johnson arrived in Edinburgh, and Boswell introduced him to his wife. She did not like him, or his irregular hours, or his uncouth habits, such as turning candles upside-down to make them burn brighter, and dropping wax on the carpet. 'I have seen many a bear led by a man,' she complained to Boswell, 'but I never before saw a man led by a bear.'

For his expedition into the wilds of Scotland, Johnson had brought a pair of pistols and a plentiful supply of powder and shot, but 'Corsica' Boswell assured him that they were unnecessary, and they left them behind. Instead they took Boswell's servant, and on 18 August they started: the old, sceptical moralist, whose 'business was with life and manners', and the young, irrepressible bounder, whose business was with everything save 'the beauties of Nature'. They drove in a chaise up the east coast to Aberdeen, where Johnson was presented with the freedom of the town. His worst fears were realized: there were dried haddocks for breakfast, the windows would not open, and the country 'grew more stony, and continued equally naked of all vegetable

From 'A Poetical and Congratulatory Epistle to James
Boswell Esq. on his Journal of a Tour to the Hebrides,
with the Celebrated Doctor Johnson.' By Peter Pindar.

Sweet is thy page, I ween, that doth recite,
How thou and Johnson arm in arm one night,
Marched through fair Edinburgh's Pactolian showers,
Which Cloacina bountifully pours:
How sweetly grumbled, too, was Sam's remark,
'I smell you, master Bozzy, in the dark!' . . .
I mark the brown great-coat of cloth he wore,
That two huge Patagonian pockets bore . . .
How are we all with rapture touch'd to see
Where, when, and at what hour, you swallowed tea . . .
I see thee stuffing, with a hand uncouth,
An old dried whiting in thy Johnson's mouth;
And lo! I see, with all his might and main,
Thy Johnson spit the whiting out again.

Johnson walking in the Hebrides (*left*)

'A considerable protuberance.' Ben Nevis. ▶

decoration'. At Forres they drove across the very heath where Macbeth met the witches, and at Inverness they entered the Highlands, 'a country upon which perhaps no wheel has ever rolled'. They now mounted horses – 'Dr Johnson rode very well' – and, accompanied by two Highlanders on foot, rode south-west along the shore of Loch Ness, before striking west into the mountains. Here, at one of their inns, Johnson gave the landlord's daughter a present of *Cocker's Arithmetic*, which he had read on the way. 'An eye accustomed to flowery pastures and waving harvests,' he noted, 'is astonished and repelled by this wide extent of hopeless sterility;' and he rebuked Boswell when he called a mountain 'immense': 'No,' he said, 'it is no more than a considerable protuberance.'

On reaching the coast, they sailed to Skye, and began a series of visits to hospitable Hebrideans. The weather was wet and stormy, and on one boisterous sail Johnson's spurs were lost overboard. 'There was something wild,' he observed, 'in letting a pair of spurs be carried into the sea out of a boat.' At Kingsburgh they met the celebrated Flora Macdonald, who had helped the Young Pretender to escape in 1746, and Johnson slept in the Prince's bed. It rained, he had a cold, and Miss M'Leod knitted him a large flannel night cap. He disliked flannel, for 'animal substances are less cleanly than vegetable'. 'I have often thought,' he said, 'that if I kept a seraglio, the ladies should all wear linen gowns.' Boswell was convulsed with laughter, but crushed by a broadside of degrading images, and when he got hopelessly drunk a few nights later expected another onslaught; but the Doctor was in good humour, and that evening toyed with one of the married ladies, who sat on his knee and kissed him.

The weather was atrocious, and when they sailed for Mull, they were caught in a great storm. Johnson was sick, and retired under cover; Boswell lasted a little longer, feared the ship would split, catch fire, or blow up, but recollection of Ogden's *Sermons on Prayer*, and an order to hold a piece of rope, restored his confidence.

So far Johnson had been philosophical and patient, but now he became querulous: 'This is a waste of life,' he complained. 'O, Sir, a most dolorous country.' Moreover, he lost his large oak walking-stick, and was convinced that it had been stolen. 'It is not to be expected that any man in Mull, who has got it, will part with it. Consider, Sir, the value of such a *piece of timber* here!' However, he allowed himself to be dragged to Iona, where Boswell felt himself a reformed character, but the disillusioned Rambler's peculiar accuracy of observation detected much fiction in the legends of that holy island.

At last, on 2 November, they reached Auchinleck, where Boswell, not without anxiety, introduced his companion, the Tory High Churchman, to

'To see Dr Samuel Johnson . . .
salute Miss Flora Macdonald in the
Isle of Skye was a striking sight.'
(*Boswell*)

'His object was to keep me out of
the way of those who were busy
working the vessel.' (*Boswell*)

Lord Auchinleck, Boswell's father.

his father, the Whig Presbyterian. The two men, both of an age, managed to keep the peace for a few days, but a mention of Cromwell sparked off the explosion. Boswell draws a veil, but we have the old laird's opinion of the Doctor, at least according to Sir Walter Scott, a child of two at the time: 'There's nae hope for Jamie, mon; Jamie is gaen clean gyte. . . . Whose tail do you think he's pinned himself to now, mon? – A dominie, mon – an auld dominie – he keeped a schule and caauld it an acaademy.'

Johnson c. 1773, painted by Reynolds for the Streatham library.

'Dr Johnson and my father came in collision . . . yet I durst not interfere.' (*Boswell*)

Goldsmith's monument in Westminster Abbey, by Joseph Nollekens; with Johnson's Latin epitaph.

OLIVARII GOLDSMITH
Poetæ, Physici, Historici,
qui nullum fere scribendi genus
non tetigit,
nullum quod tetigit non ornavit;
sive risus essent movendi,
sive lacrimæ,
affectuum potens, at lenis dominator,
ingenio sublimis, vividus, versatilis,
oratione grandis, nitidus, venustus,

Hoc monumento memoriam coluit
Sodalium amor,
Amicorum fides,
Lectorum veneratio.
Natus Hibernia, Forneiæ Lonfordiensis
in loco cui nomen Pallas,
Nov. XXIX. MDCCXXXI.
Eblanæ literis institutus,
Objit Londini,
Apr. IV. MDCCLXXIV.

Soon after Johnson's return to London, Goldsmith died. 'Dr Goldsmith was my last hero,' he told Mrs Thrale, and in a letter to Langton wrote, 'He died of a fever, exasperated, as I believe, by the fear of distress. He had raised money and squandered it by every artifice of acquisition and folly of expense. But let not his frailties be remembered; he was a very great man.' He composed a Latin epitaph for the monument in Westminster Abbey, and sent it to the Club for approval. The feeling was that an English epitaph would be more appropriate, but as nobody had the courage to tell Johnson, it was decided to send him a round-robin. Johnson received it good-humouredly, but insisted that he would 'never consent to disgrace the walls of Westminster Abbey with an English inscription'. The Latin epitaph, therefore, with its famous phrase, 'Nullum quod tetigit non ornavit' – 'He touched nothing that he did not adorn' – was engraved on the monument.

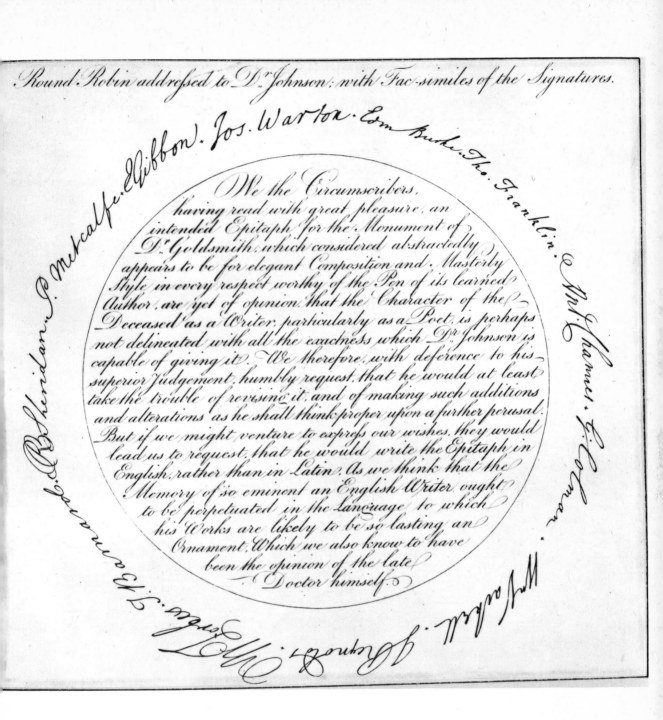

Round Robin addressed to Dr. Johnson; with Fac-similes of the Signatures.

We the Circumscribers,
having read with great pleasure, an
intended Epitaph for the Monument of
Dr. Goldsmith; which considered abstractedly
appears to be for elegant Composition and Masterly
Style in every respect worthy of the Pen of its learned
Author, are yet of opinion, that the Character of the
Deceased as a Writer, particularly as a Poet, is perhaps
not delineated with all the exactness which Dr. Johnson is
capable of giving it. We therefore, with deference to his
superior Judgement, humbly request, that he would at least
take the trouble of revising it, and of making such additions
and alterations as he shall think proper, upon a further perusal.
But if we might venture to express our wishes, they would
lead us to request, that he would write the Epitaph in
English, rather than in Latin. As we think that the
Memory of so eminent an English Writer ought
to be perpetuated in the Language to which
his Works are likely to be so lasting an
Ornament. Which we also know to have
been the opinion of the late
Doctor himself.

Bennet Langton, a classical scholar, refused to sign
the round-robin suggesting that Goldsmith's epitaph be in English.

93

Anna Seward (1747–1809). 'Johnson . . . the most wonderful composition of great and absurd, of misanthropy and benevolence, of luminous intellect and prejudiced darkness, that was ever produced in the human breast.'

(*below*) 'He that has seen Dovedale has no need to visit the Highlands.' (Johnson's *Diary*, 16 July 1774)

'We climbed with great labour. I was breathless and harrassed.' (*Diary*, 26 August 1774) Peter Pindar's friend, Richard Wilson, painted this view of Snowdon at about this time. ▶

In the summer of this year, 1774, the Thrales took Johnson to Wales, Hester's native country, and with them went their eldest daughter 'Queeney', as Johnson called her, a girl of ten. They travelled comfortably by carriage, and stopped at Lichfield on the way. Although so short-sighted, Johnson had an eye for a lady's dress, and when 'my mistress' appeared in a morning nightgown and close cap, he sent her back to change into something gayer. They called on Lucy Porter, now a wealthy spinster, having inherited a fortune from her brother, Johnson's stepson. They breakfasted with eccentric Erasmus Darwin, and supped with Peter Garrick, but Johnson went alone to see Anna Seward, the 'Swan of Lichfield', whose father had succeeded Walmesley in the Palace. She wrote verses and letters, in which Johnson appeared as 'the old elephant', whose passion for Mrs Thrale was largely cupboard love. He trembled whenever he saw Anna: she was so like her grandfather, his old headmaster, John Hunter.

They stayed in splendour with Taylor at Ashbourne, and then drove to Chester and North Wales. Johnson loved travelling in a carriage, as the company could not leave him, and the motion improved his hearing: 'but the carriage must stop sometime, and the people must come home at last'. He became impatient when Hester could not hear him above the noise of the wheels, and she complained that she had to be civil for all four.

She wrote a journal: 'Johnson's birthplace filled my mind with emotion.' But she was not in high spirits: she was pregnant, as usual, and Queeney kept her awake with a bad cough and worms. Johnson also kept a diary, mainly matter-of-fact: '*Tuesday, 5th July*. We left Streatham 11 a.m. Price of four horses two shillings a mile. Barnet 1.40 p.m. On the road read Tully's epistles.' But at Bodvel, Hester's birthplace near Caernarvon, he wrote sympathetically: 'Mrs Thrale remembered the rooms, and wandered over them, with recollection of her childhood. This species of pleasure is always melancholy. The walk was cut down and the pond was dry. Nothing was better.'

Their last stop was at Beaconsfield with Burke, who came home late, 'very much flustered with liquor'. Parliament had been suddenly dissolved; there was to be an election, and Thrale told Hester that they must return to the Brewery House, instead of to her beloved Streatham. 'I must be shut up in that odious dungeon,' she concluded her journal, 'where nobody will come near me, the children are to be sick for want of air, and I am never to see a face but Mr Johnson's.' She was tired and disappointed, for a few days earlier she had written: 'Mr Johnson is on every occasion so very kind, feels friendship so acutely, and expresses it so delicately, that it is wonderfully flattering to me to have his company.' Johnson had enjoyed himself, though he found Wales 'so little different from England that it offers nothing to the speculation of the traveller.'

In 1775 he published his *Journey to the Western Islands of Scotland*. His style was now less laboured, and of the Aberdeen granite (with which the streets of London were being paved) it is good to read: 'It is beautiful, and must be very lasting.' When at Auchinleck a gentleman had asked him how he liked the Highlands, he had answered, 'Who *can* like the Highlands?' and his book, mainly descriptive of life and manners, was attacked by a number of Scots, jealous for their country; though the verdict of Lord Chief Justice Mansfield, a Scot, was that Johnson 'spoke ill of nobody but Ossian'.

Ossian was a legendary third-century Irish bard, ancient manuscripts of whose poems James Macpherson professed to have found, and these, he asserted, were the originals of his *Fingal*, an epic poem, translated from the Gaelic into his romantic English prose. The sceptical Johnson did not believe him, and said so, and Macpherson wrote a threatening letter, to which Johnson replied:

I received your foolish and impudent letter. Any violence offered me I shall do my best to repel; and what I cannot do for myself, the law shall do for me. I hope I shall never be deterred from detecting what I think a cheat, by the menaces of a ruffian.

James Macpherson (1736–96) (*left*). 'I thought your book an imposture; I think it an imposture still.' Dr Thomas Percy, later Bishop of Dromore (1729–1811) (*right*). 'A man out of whose company I never go without having learned something.'

He bought a large oak stick, and heard no more from Macpherson.

Johnson was the principal pillar of the classical school that had been estab-lished by Dryden and by Pope, who maintained that the proper study of man-kind is man; that the town, therefore, is more important than the country; that reason should restrain and regulate the imagination, and that in poetry emotion is best confined within the bars of the heroic couplet. He disliked the romanti-cism of *Fingal*, and therefore it was a fraud, as were the 'Rowley' poems of Chatterton; and he made fun of the romanticism of his friends Thomas Percy and Thomas Warton, the first of whom published a collection of old ballads as *Reliques of Ancient English Poetry*, the other a *History of English Poetry*, a rediscovery of the Middle Ages and the Elizabethans, notably Spenser. Johnson mocked:

> *Thus I spoke, and speaking sigh'd;*
> *Scarce repress'd the starting tear;*
> *When the smiling sage reply'd,*
> *'Come, my lad, and drink some beer.'*

And again:

> *Phrase that time has flung away;*
> *Uncouth words in disarray,*
> *Trick'd in ancient ruff and bonnet,*
> *Ode, and elegy, and sonnet.*

Even Boswell, however, could not approve of his *Taxation No Tyranny*, a pamphlet that Johnson wrote in support of the government's policy of taxing the American colonists without their consent, a policy that led to the War of Independence which began this year. Johnson, the old Tory, saw the threatened revolution as the upsetting of the established order, and for him the upsetters were 'a race of convicts, and ought to be thankful for anything we allow them short of hanging'. Politically he was an anachronism: 'Were I in power, I would turn out every man who dared to oppose me.' Yet it should be remembered that he detested slavery, and asked, 'How is it that we hear the loudest yelps for liberty among the drivers of negroes?'

It was now that he received the degree of Doctor of Laws from Oxford University, but, although known everywhere as Dr Johnson, he seems never to have assumed the title himself, preferring plain Mr Johnson or, better still, the gentility of Esquire.

To France with the Thrales

On 14 September he wrote to Boswell, casually mentioning that he was to set out the next day on another journey. The journey was to France, his only trip abroad, and the party the same as that of the previous year, with the addition of Queeney's tutor, Baretti. On the 18th he wrote to Levet from Calais, and a month later from Paris: 'We have been today at Versailles' – 'a mean town', he noted in his journal. 'We came yesterday from Fontainebleau' – 'a

'The shops of Paris are mean.'

(*left*) View from the old grain market looking towards Pont Notre-Dame.

(*below*) The Gate of St Denis.

large mean town'. 'We went to see the King and Queen at dinner, and the Queen was so impressed by Miss [Queeney] that she sent one of the Gentlemen to enquire who she was.' On the way to Paris there had been an accident: one of the carriages got out of control, and Mr Thrale leaped into a chalkpit, from which he merged 'looking *as white!*' Johnson was unsympathetic: accidents did not happen. In another respect he was a disappointing travelling companion. Mr Thrale loved prospects, fine views, but Johnson had no use for 'such nonsense; a blade of grass is always a blade of grass, whether in one country or another. Let us, if we do talk, talk about something. Men and women are my subjects of inquiry.' He noted that the French have no laws for the maintenance of their poor, sent his compliments to Miss Williams, his love to Francis, and later summed up his impression of France in conversation with Boswell.

> 'The great in France live very magnificently, but the rest very miserably.' [It was fourteen years before the Revolution.]
> There is no happy middle state as in England. The shops of Paris are mean; the meat in the markets is such as would be sent to a jail in England; and Mr Thrale justly observed that the cookery of the French was forced upon them by necessity, for they could not eat their meat unless they added some taste to it. The French are an indelicate people; they will spit upon any place. At Madame [du Boccage]'s, a literary lady of rank, the footman took the sugar in his fingers, and threw it into my coffee. I was going to put it aside; but hearing it was made on purpose for me, I e'en tasted Tom's fingers. The same lady would needs make tea *à l'anglaise*. The spout of the teapot did not pour freely; she bade the footman blow into it. France is worse than Scotland in everything but climate. Nature has done more for the French; but they have done less for themselves than the Scotch have done.

However, the holiday had proved such a success that they decided to go to Italy next year. 'A man who has not been in Italy,' Johnson observed, 'is always conscious of an inferiority.'

Bolt Court   When Boswell arrived in London in March 1776, he found that Johnson had moved house again, to Number 8 Bolt Court, still near his beloved Fleet Street. He was preparing to go off on his annual jaunt to the Midlands, 'And you, Boswell,' he said, 'shall go with me.' One of their companions in the Oxford coach was the architect John Gwynne, to whom Johnson expounded the nature of his art. Ornamental architecture, he explained, consumes labour disproportionate to its utility. In much the same way, sculpture is not worth the labour involved, though painting may be.

In Oxford they called on Dr Adams, now Master of Pembroke College, and spent an evening with Thomas Warton of Trinity, where they talked of

No. 8 Bolt Court, Fleet Street. Johnson's house from 1776 until his death. ▶

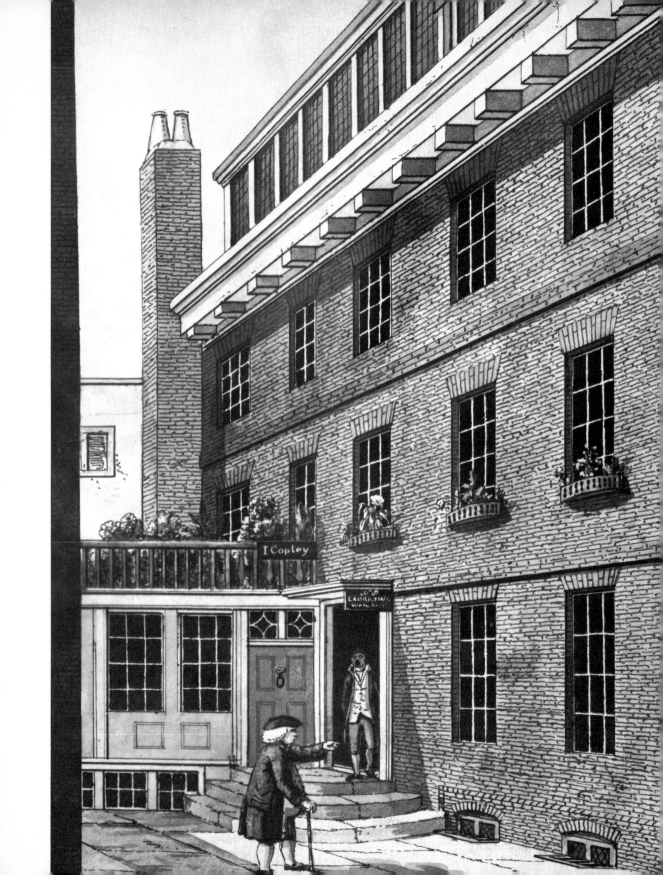

'We rode through Blenheim Park. I looked at the magnificent bridge built by John Duke of Marlborough, over a small rivulet . . . and saw that now, by the genius of Brown, a magnificent body of water was collected.' (*Boswell*, 21 March 1776)

Lucy Porter, Johnson's stepdaughter, 'now an old maid'.

biography, which, said Johnson, is rarely well executed. The next day, as they drove through Blenheim Park, recently laid out by 'Capability' Brown, Boswell was moved to say, 'You and I, Sir, have, I think, seen together the extremes of what can be seen in Britain – the wild rough island of Mull, and Blenheim Park.' They dined at an excellent inn, where Johnson spoke in praise of the English tavern, and with great emotion the lonely old widower repeated Shenstone's lines:

> Whoe'er has travell'd life's dull round,
> Where'er his stages may have been,
> May sigh to think he still has found
> The warmest welcome at an inn.

After dinner, as they drove rapidly along in their post-chaise, Johnson remarked contentedly: 'Life has not many things better than this.' One thing was better than driving with Boswell: 'Driving briskly in a post-chaise with a pretty woman.'

'Sir, I should as soon have thought of building
a man of war, as of collecting such a museum.'
Richard Green's museum at Lichfield.

In Birmingham they met Hector and his sister, a widow who was, Johnson confided, the first woman he loved. At Lichfield they put up at the Three Crowns, next door to Johnson's birthplace, and Boswell met Peter Garrick, Anna Seward, Miss Elizabeth Aston and her sister Mrs Gaskell, widow of the notorious parson who, with gothick barbarity, had cut down Shakespeare's mulberry tree at Stratford. Then, of course, there was Lucy Porter, 'now an old maid with much simplicity of manner', and it was while breakfasting with her that Johnson received a letter to say that the Thrales had lost their only surviving son: 'One of the most dreadful things that has happened in my time.' He decided to cut short his visit to Ashbourne, and return to London to comfort his friends. That night, however, they made merry, and went to see Garrick's *Stratford Jubilee* at the Town Hall, where Johnson confessed that forty years ago he had fallen in love with an actress. Their levity made Boswell feel guilty, but Johnson reassured him: 'I would not have you be gay in the presence of the distressed, . . . but you may be gay at a distance.'

Bath. 'I had never seen that beautiful city, and wished to take the opportunity of visiting it while Johnson was there.' (*Boswell*)

Next day Dr Taylor sent, as Boswell put it, 'an equipage suited to a wealthy well-beneficed clergyman', which took them to Ashbourne. Boswell found Taylor more like a hearty English squire than a clergyman, and wondered at Johnson's friendship with this bucolic Whig. They stayed only two nights, but when they arrived in London, Johnson was vexed to find Mrs Thrale just starting for Bath. It was no way to treat a friend who had hastened to console a distressed mother.

On Good Friday, Boswell attended morning service with Johnson, who slumbered through the sermon, and on the way home he introduced the subject of fornication. He received no comfort. 'I would punish it much more than it is done,' said Johnson, 'and so restrain it.' Soon after this, he joined the Thrales in Bath, and a few days later Boswell followed. The Italian holiday was off, and Johnson was to have no more protracted tours.

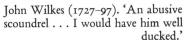

John Wilkes (1727–97). 'An abusive scoundrel . . . I would have him well ducked.'

It was after their return to London that Boswell inveigled Johnson into meeting John Wilkes, the personification of all that Johnson detested: a profligate free-thinker and demagogic Whig, who had won popularity as a champion of liberty. The occasion was a dinner given by the booksellers, the Dilly brothers. When Johnson entered the room he found most of the company strangers. 'Who is that gentleman?' he asked. 'Mr Arthur Lee.' 'Too, too, too,' he muttered, for the man was an American. 'And who is the gentleman in lace?' 'Mr Wilkes, Sir.' On hearing this, Johnson retired to a window-seat with a book, but when dinner was served he found Wilkes next to him. Despite his squint, Wilkes was a charmer, and knew how to subdue Johnson: 'Pray give me leave, Sir,' he said, helping him to veal; 'it is better here – a little of the brown – some fat, Sir – a little of the stuffing – some gravy – let me have the pleasure of giving you some butter – allow me to recommend a squeeze of this orange – or the lemon, perhaps, may have more zest.' After a surly acknowledgement, Johnson was soon reduced to complacency. At least they agreed about Scotland, and, turning to Wilkes, Johnson said of Boswell, 'He lives among savages in Scotland, and among rakes in London.' 'Except,' Wilkes replied, 'when he is with grave, sober, decent people, like you and me.' 'And we ashamed of him,' added Johnson with a smile. Boswell had the satisfaction of hearing Johnson tell Miss Williams how much he had been pleased with Wilkes's company.

In spite of excursions and diversions, Johnson was still a prey to melancholy and anxiety. 'When I survey my past life,' he wrote in his *Meditations* on Easter Day 1777, 'I discover nothing but a barren waste of time, with some disorders of body, and disturbances of mind, very near to madness.' And he composed a prayer: 'Have mercy upon me, O God, have mercy upon me; years and infirmities oppress me; terror and anxiety beset me.' However, he now had work to distract him, and in May wrote to Boswell: 'I am engaged to write little Lives, and little Prefaces, to a little Edition of the English Poets.' The work was commissioned by a number of publishers who planned to bring out a uniform edition of English poets, and agreed to pay Johnson two hundred guineas for his contribution. He might have asked, and received, five times as much, had he written only for money.

At the end of August he went to stay with Taylor at Ashbourne, where he was joined a fortnight later by Boswell. Boswell was interested in Taylor's opinion of Johnson: 'He is a man of a very clear head, great power of words,

'We went to the church of Ashbourne, which is one of the largest and most luminous that I have seen in any town of the same size.' (*Boswell*, 21 September 1777)

'He [Reynolds] may paint himself as deaf if he chooses, but I will not be *blinking Sam*.'

and a very gay imagination; but there is no disputing with him. He will not hear you, and having a louder voice than you, must roar you down.' He was equally interested in Johnson's opinion of Taylor: 'Sir, I love him, but my regard for him does not increase. As it is said in the Apocrypha,' – he had just read the book for the first time – ' "His talk is of bullocks." I do not suppose he is very fond of my company. His habits are by no means sufficiently clerical: this he knows that I see; and no man likes to live under the eye of perpetual disapprobation.' One evening he was able to record a clash between the roaring Tory and bellowing Whig. In a violent argument with his Whig friend, Johnson grew so outrageous as to maintain that if the people of England had their way, the Hanoverian George III would be sent away that night, and his adherents hanged next morning. This roused Taylor to a pitch of bellowing, and an assertion that the Stuarts were generally abhorred by the English. No wonder Johnson was glad to accept an invitation to dine with Dr Butter of Derby, and Taylor equally glad to see him go.

Boswell stayed ten days at Ashbourne, and on the evening before his departure for Scotland was in a receptive, sentimental mood. Three guests entertained them with tunes on the fiddle, and Boswell, who could also play, confessed that music moved him to alternate sensations of pathetic dejection and daring resolution, so that he was ready to rush into the thickest part of a battle. 'Sir, I should never hear it,' said Johnson, 'if it made me such a fool.'

Happily, the seeds of another friendship had been sown that spring. In March, Mrs Thrale, followed later by Johnson, visited Dr Charles Burney,

Fanny Burney

Dr Charles Burney (1726–1814). 'Dr Johnson was remarkably fond of Dr Burney's *History of Music*.' (*Frances Reynolds*)

Fanny Burney (1752–1840), author of *Evelina*, 1778. 'There is none like you, my dear little Burney!' ▶

who had just published the first volume of his *History of Music*. His daughters were there, and one of them, Fanny, aged twenty-four, described the occasion in a letter.

Dr Johnson was announced. He is, indeed, very ill-favoured; is tall and stout; but stoops terribly; he is almost bent double. His mouth is almost continually opening and shutting, as if he was chewing. He has a strange method of frequently twirling his fingers, and twisting his hands. His body is in continual agitation, *see-sawing* up and down; his feet are never a moment quiet; and, in short, his whole person is in *perpetual motion*. His dress, too, . . . was as much out of the common road as his figure; he had a large wig, snuff-colour coat, and gold buttons, but no ruffles to his shirt, and black worsted stockings. He is shockingly near-sighted and did not, till she held out her hand to him, even know Mrs Thrale.

To the company's dismay, he made at once for the books, for 'it seems he is the most silent creature, when not particularly drawn out'. There was music, and talk of Bach, and at last Johnson entered the conversation with, 'And pray, Sir, *who is Bach? Is he a piper?*'

In January 1778 Fanny Burney's novel *Evelina* was published anonymously. It was a tremendous success; everybody was reading it, and trying to discover the author. Johnson pronounced that Richardson would have been proud to have written it, and that Harry Fielding had never created such characters. In July Dr Burney told Mrs Thrale that 'our Fanny' was the author; Mrs Thrale told Johnson, and in August Fanny was invited to Streatham, 'the most consequential day of my life'. Mrs Thrale was sweet, amiable and charming, and at dinner Fanny sat between her and Johnson, who said, 'Sitting by Miss Burney makes me very proud today.' So began the friendship between the seventy-year-old 'Lexiphanes' and young Fanny Burney. Her visits became more frequent and more prolonged, until she spent most of her time at Streatham. She liked Mrs Thrale more and more, for her kindness, benevolence and gaiety reminded her of her father, and Johnson was always loath to part with 'my little Burney'.

It is good to see Johnson in such domestic happiness. 'In the evening he was as lively and full of wit and sport as I have ever seen him,' wrote Fanny, 'and Mrs Thrale and I had him quite to ourselves; for Mr Thrale came in from giving an election dinner so tired, that he neither opened his eyes nor mouth, but fell fast asleep. Indeed, after tea he generally does.' Another evening, at a party, Johnson stopped her, and asked how she did. 'I was afraid,' she cried, 'you did not intend to know me again, for you have not spoken to me since your return from town.' 'My dear,' he replied, taking both her hands, 'I was not sure of you, I am so near-sighted.' Then drawing her towards him, he kissed her. 'No, my darling! – my dear little Burney, when I give you up——' 'What then, Sir?' asked Mrs Thrale. 'Why, I don't know; for whoever could give her up would deserve worse than I can say.'

When Boswell arrived in London that spring, he found the room that had been allotted to him at Bolt Court occupied by three more of Johnson's dependants: Mrs Desmoulins, her daughter, and a Miss Poll Carmichael. In addition, Johnson gave Mrs Desmoulins half a guinea a week, a fair proportion of his income. On Good Friday she acted as hostess at breakfast, after which Johnson and Boswell went to morning service. On their way back, a decent-looking elderly man accosted Johnson, and asked if he remembered him, saying he had been at Pembroke College with him fifty years before, and that his name was Edwards. 'You are a philosopher, Dr Johnson,' he said. 'I have tried too in my time to be a philosopher; but, I don't know how, cheerfulness was always breaking in.'

Johnson had need of all the cheerfulness he could muster. 'Williams hates everybody,' he wrote to Mrs Thrale on one of his visits to Bolt Court. 'Levet hates Desmoulins, and does not love Williams; Desmoulins hates them both;

'That stroke of death which has eclipsed the gaiety of nations.' The monument to David Garrick, by Henry Webber, in Westminster Abbey.

Poll loves none of them.' And to Boswell in November: 'My health is not restored, my nights are restless and tedious.'

Then in January 1779 he lost one of his oldest friends, David Garrick. *Death of Garrick* 'What are the hopes of man?' he asked. 'I am disappointed by that stroke of death which has eclipsed the gaiety of nations, and impoverished the public stock of harmless pleasure.' A year later he lost one of his youngest friends, Topham Beauclerk. 'Poor dear Beauclerk,' he wrote to Boswell. 'His wit and his folly, his acuteness and maliciousness, his merriment and reasoning, are now over. Such another will not often be found among mankind.' He added, 'Poor Mr Thrale has been in extreme danger from an apoplectical disorder.'

Poor Mr Thrale was in Bath, recuperating after a stroke, or rather gorging himself into another one, as Mrs Thrale wrote to Johnson in April 1780: 'He looks well enough, but I have no notion of health for a man whose mouth cannot be sewed up. Burney and I and Queeney tease him every meal he eats, . . . but what *can* one do? He will eat, I think, and if he does eat I know he will not live.'

'I walked with Dr Scot to look at Newgate, and found it in ruins, with the fire yet glowing.' The Gordon, or 'No Popery', Riots of June 1780.

'There was something slouching in the gait and dress of Mr Boswell.' (*Fanny Burney*)

'Mr Thrale had removed to a house in Grosvenor Square.' (*Boswell*) (*right*)

'We stopped a little while by the rails of the Adelphi, looking on the Thames, and I said to him with some emotion that I was now thinking of two friends we had lost, who once lived in the buildings behind us, Beauclerk and Garrick. "Ay, Sir, (said he tenderly) and two such friends as cannot be supplied."' (*Boswell*, 20 April 1781)

It was at the Thrales in the previous year that Fanny Burney first met Boswell. He spoke with a strong Scottish accent, and seemed unconsciously to imitate the manner of Johnson, who treated him fondly as a schoolboy. When they sat at table, Boswell, as of right, took the chair next to Johnson, but was asked to move, as the seat was Miss Burney's. Reluctantly he took another chair, and placed it behind Johnson's, and when the great man began to speak, his eyes goggled, his mouth dropped open, and he leaned forward to catch every syllable. Johnson, thinking he was at the other end of the table, made some friendly remark to 'Bozzy', but, when answered from behind his back, clapped his hand upon his knee, and demanded, 'What do you there, Sir? Go to the table, Sir!' Boswell obeyed. After a time, however, he rose to fetch something from another room; but Johnson saw him and called, 'What are you thinking of, Sir? Running about in the middle of meals! Come back to your place, Sir!'

He was still writing *The Lives of the English Poets*, and would sometimes produce proof-sheets at breakfast for the Thrales and Fanny to discuss. Frank Barber was collecting them for Boswell, but when Fanny hinted that she would treasure one, Johnson offered her a whole Life, adding with a smile, 'Choose your poet.' Without hesitation she chose Pope.

'Lives of the Poets'

Johnson knew that life is more important than art, and it followed that biography was one of the most important forms of literature: the portrait of a man as he really was, the re-creation of a life and mind. He took little interest in accuracy of fact and detail, but drew on his own seventy years' experience of life and reading, writing hastily, rarely referring to books, and fearlessly giving his considered opinion of a man and his work. He was sometimes blinded by prejudice, but his praise meant all the more. He did not like Milton, the puritan republican: he did not like the make-believe of the pastoral convention, and therefore disliked *Lycidas*; he preferred rhyme to blank verse, yet he wrote of 'that wonderful performance' *Paradise Lost*: 'I cannot prevail on myself to wish that Milton had been a rhymer, for I cannot wish his work to be other than it is.'

His *Life of Lord Lyttleton* brought him into conflict with the aristocratic Elizabeth Montagu, whose great house in Portman Square was the centre of the blue-stocking intellectuals. Johnson had written: 'Lord Lyttleton's poems . . . have nothing to be despised, and little to be admired.' It was very true, but Lyttleton had been a friend of Mrs Montagu, and as a result she dropped Johnson, at least for a time. 'There are people whom one should like very well to drop, but would not wish to be dropped by,' he remarked ruefully.

The Lives of the English Poets, perhaps the most valuable of Johnson's works, was completed in March 1781, when Boswell, fresh from Scotland, met him walking along Fleet Street, or rather rolling along, for his motion seemed to be

Mrs Thrale's breakfast-table at the Brewery House.

independent of his legs. They called on Henry Thrale, now in Grosvenor Square, and Boswell found him sadly changed in appearance. A few days later he died in convulsions, brought on by over-eating. 'I felt almost the last flutter of his pulse,' wrote Johnson in his *Meditations*, 'and looked for the last time upon the face that for fifteen years had never been turned upon me but with respect or benignity.'

The death of Henry Thrale meant more than the loss of a friend; it was a threat to the life that Johnson had lived for the last fifteen years: of a home at Streatham, surrounded by every luxury, with servants and carriages always at his disposal. For the moment, however, he was happy in his duties as one of the executors, bustling about with an inkhorn and pen in his buttonhole, arranging the sale of the Anchor Brewery. 'We are not here to sell a parcel of boilers and vats,' he boasted, 'but the potentiality of growing rich beyond the dreams of avarice.' The brewery was bought by David Barclay, a Quaker banker, and Thrale's chief clerk, John Perkins, was taken into partnership.

Death of Henry Thrale

Deed of Sale by which the Thrale Brewery became 'Barclay and Perkins'.

'The potentiality of growing rich beyond the dreams of avarice.' The Thrale Brewery. (*below*)

Luton Hoo (*below right*). 'This is one of the places I do not regret having come to see.'

Yet Johnson was uneasy. Hester Thrale was only forty, an attractive, wealthy and eminently marriageable widow, for whom, despite his years, he felt more than a paternal affection, and he was disturbed by the presence of Gabriele Piozzi, a distinguished Italian musician, at Streatham. The Thrales had met Piozzi at a musical party given by Dr Burney, and according to Fanny he was 'a first-rate singer, whose voice was deliciously sweet'. Mrs Thrale agreed, and for the last year or so he had been employed as Queeney's music master. However, he went abroad in July, and Johnson, after accompanying Boswell on his Scottish journey as far as Luton Hoo in Bedfordshire, returned to Streatham, before making his annual pilgrimage to the Midlands. At Ashbourne he heard that Piozzi was returning to Streatham, and wrote to Hester: 'When *he* comes and I come, you will have two about you that love you; and I question if either of us heartily cares how few more you have. But how many soever they may be, I hope you keep your kindness for me.' He hurried back, only to find Miss Williams and Mrs Desmoulins ill at Bolt Court, and early in the New Year he lost Robert Levet, the man whom he had resolved to keep always about him, however his way of life might be changed. His death inspired the most poignant of his poems:

> Well tried through many a varying year,
>   See Levet to the grave descend;
> Officious, innocent, sincere,
>   Of every friendless name the friend. . . .

> His virtues walk'd their narrow round,
>   Nor made a pause, nor left a void;
> And sure the eternal Master found
>   His single talent well employ'd.

Johnson, Hester Thrale and Gabriele Piozzi. 'Do not, do not drive me from you, for I have not deserved either neglect or hatred.'

Farewell to Streatham   It was an unhappy beginning to an unhappy year. He was ill. 'Here is Mr Johnson very ill indeed,' wrote Hester in February. 'If I lose him I am more than undone: friend, father, guardian, confidant.' A visit to Oxford did little to cure his asthma; on his return to Streatham he felt he was less welcome than before, and back at Bolt Court he wrote to implore Hester not to let 'Mr Piozzi, nor anybody else, put me quite out of your head'. In the autumn Hester let Streatham Place, and Johnson prayed 'that I may with humble and sincere thankfulness remember the comforts and conveniences which I have enjoyed at this place,' packed his bundles, said farewell to the house and library, and set off with Hester and her daughters for Brighton, where Fanny Burney joined them.

Fanny knew the cause of her friend's changed attitude to Johnson, for Hester had told her of her passion for Piozzi, thought some years later she was to give a different reason:

Veneration for his virtues, reverence for his talents, delight in his conversation, and habitual endurance of a yoke my husband first put upon me, and of which he contentedly bore his share for sixteen or seventeen years, made me go on so long with Mr Johnson; but the perpetual confinement I will

own to have been terrifying in the first years of our friendship, and irksome in the last; nor could I pretend to support it without help, when my coadjutor was no more.

Hester, with visions of a new romantic life with the man she loved, was making excuses for her coming break with Johnson. He was suspicious, and suspicion combined with illness made him so irritable that Brighton society excluded him from their invitations. 'He has been in a terrible severe humour of late,' wrote Fanny, 'and has really frightened all the people, till they almost run from him.'

In November they all returned to London, where Hester had taken a house in Argyll Street, and there Boswell found Johnson on his arrival from Scotland in March 1783. He looked pale, and his breathing distressed him, but after dinner and a rest he began to talk so triumphantly that Boswell turned to Hester: 'O, for shorthand to take this down!' 'You'll carry it all in your head;' she replied, 'a long head is as good as short hand.' On 5 April Johnson returned to Bolt Court and his two sick old ladies. He was never to see his 'dear mistress' again.

Hester was in a state of hysterical indecision. When she told the eighteen-year-old Queeney of her love for Piozzi, and asked for her approval of her marriage, she was accused of sacrificing her daughters for her own selfish ends. Fanny Burney went even further, protesting that she was abandoning her 'children, religion, situation, country and character', and society agreed. Yet her daughters were provided for, Johnson was one of their guardians, and there was no reason why she should not marry Piozzi. At length, however, she accepted the verdict of society, and on 6 April said farewell to Piozzi, who returned to Italy, while she withdrew to Bath, 'where I knew Mr Johnson would not follow me'.

Boswell good-naturedly put up with Johnson's irritability, and of necessity with his cat Hodge, for he disliked cats so much that he felt uneasy if one was in the room. On 26 May he found Fanny Burney taking tea with him, and spent much of the 29th at Bolt Court, as he was to start for Scotland on the next day. Johnson embraced him on parting, and Boswell left him with a fearful apprehension of what might happen before he returned.

Last illness   Johnson was well enough to sit for his portrait to young John Opie, but early in the morning of 17 June he had a stroke. Fortunately, it only affected his speech, and in July he was well enough to stay with Langton at Rochester, and in August with William Bowles, near Salisbury. While there, he heard that Miss Williams had died, and he returned to the solitude of a house from which two of his oldest companions had gone. Moreover, he was afflicted not only

◄ From Brighton, Johnson visited
Cowdray. 'We see here how our
ancestors lived.'

'On Monday, the 16th [of June
1783], I sat for my picture, and
walked a considerable way with
little inconvenience.' He had a
stroke that night.

In August 1783 Johnson visited
Stonehenge and Salisbury
Cathedral (*below*): 'two eminent
monuments of art and rudeness
. . . the first essay and the last
perfection in architecture.'

Sarah Siddons. 'When Mrs Siddons came into the room there happened to be no chair ready for her, which he observing, said with a smile, "Madam, you who so often occasion want of seats to other people will the more easily excuse the want of one yourself."' (*J. P. Kemble*)

with asthma, but also with gout and a tumour. Nobody needed the consolation of companionship more than Johnson, and he was delighted when Mrs Siddons and her brother John Philip Kemble paid him a visit. Sarah Siddons had just made her name as a great tragic actress, and at Brighton Johnson had complained that all the talk was of 'that jade Siddons', instead of his beloved Fanny. The talk now was of actors and acting, and he promised that when Mrs Siddons played Queen Katharine in *Henry VIII* he would once more hobble to the theatre to see her.

To find companionship, he revived the Ivy Lane Club of more than thirty years ago, but they were melancholy meetings, for of its original members only the unclubable Hawkins and two others remained, and to ensure society for three evenings a week he formed another club at the Essex Head, off Fleet Street. For the first four months of 1784, however, asthma confined him to his house, while another disease, dropsy, began to gain ground. Boswell's arrival in May cheered him, and early in June they went to Oxford together, where Boswell recorded a conversation with Dr Adams.

JOHNSON. 'As I cannot be *sure* that I have fulfilled the conditions on which salvation is granted, I am afraid I may be one of the damned.' (looking dismally.)
ADAMS. 'What do you mean by damned?'
JOHNSON (passionately and loudly). 'Sent to Hell, Sir, and punished everlastingly.'

Dr William Adams (1706–89), Master of Pembroke College in 1775. 'I was Johnson's nominal tutor, but he was above my mark.'

Lord Chancellor Thurlow (1732–1806). 'I would prepare myself for no man in England but Lord Thurlow. When I am to meet with him, I should wish to know a day before.'

They returned to London on the 19th, dined at the Literary Club on the 22nd, and the next day Boswell saw fifteen men executed in front of Newgate Prison. Public executions were one of his favourite relaxations. On the 25th they dined with Paoli, when Boswell thought that Johnson ate too much. 'Alas,' said the General, 'see how very ill he looks; he can live but a very short time. Would you refuse any slight gratification to a man under sentence of death?' On the 27th they dined with Reynolds, when Johnson said he very much wished to go to Italy, and dreaded another English winter. Boswell, in consultation with Reynolds, had already written to Lord Chancellor Thurlow, to ask if Johnson's pension could be increased, so that he could afford to go, and on the 30th the three dined again together, and talked of the 'agreeable prospects of happiness in Italy'. Johnson, who now heard of the application for the first time, was moved to tears, and exclaimed, 'God bless you all. This is taking prodigious pains about a man.' As Boswell was to return to Scotland the next day, he accompanied Johnson in Reynolds's coach to the entry of Bolt Court.

He asked me whether I would not go with him to his house; I declined it, from an apprehension that my spirits would sink. We bade adieu to each other affectionately in the carriage. When he had got down upon the foot-pavement, he called out 'Fare you well;' and without looking back, sprung away with a kind of pathetic briskness, if I may use that expression, which seemed to indicate a struggle to conceal uneasiness, and impressed me with a foreboding of our long, long separation.

Meanwhile, in Bath, Mrs Thrale had been reduced to such a pitiable state of distress that her doctors feared that her mind, even her life, was in danger, and Queeney was compelled to relent. Piozzi was recalled, and on 30 June, the day of Boswell's parting, she wrote to Johnson, telling him that her daughters had left Bath, 'having heard that Mr Piozzi is coming back from Italy, and judging, perhaps, by our past friendship and continued correspondence, that his return would be succeeded by our marriage.' She added, 'I feel as if acting without a parent's consent till you write kindly.'

All Johnson's accumulated fury exploded in his reply. That she should prefer a foreigner, a Roman Catholic, an Italian fiddler to himself!

'He called out "Fare you well."' Boswell at the time of his 'long, long separation' from Johnson.

2nd July, 1784

Madam,

If I interpret your letter right, you are ignominiously married; if it is yet undone, let us once more talk together. If you have abandoned your children and your religion, God forgive your wickedness; if you have forfeited your fame and your country, may your folly do no further mischief! If the last act is yet to do, I who have loved you, esteemed you, reverenced you, and served you, I who long thought you the first of womankind, entreat that, before your fate is irrevocable, I may once more see you. I was, I once was, madam, most truly yours.

Sam Johnson.

I will come down, if you permit it.

Mrs Thrale was not to be bullied, and replied with spirit:

July 4th, 1784

Sir,

I have this morning received from you so rough a letter in reply to one which was both tenderly and respectfully written, that I am forced to desire the conclusion of a correspondence which I can bear to continue no longer. The birth of my second husband is not meaner than that of my first; his sentiments are not meaner; his profession is not meaner; and his superiority in what he professes acknowledged by all mankind. . . . To hear that I have forfeited my fame is indeed the greatest insult I ever yet received. . . . Never did I oppose your will, or control your wish; nor can your unmerited severity itself lessen my regard; but till you have changed your opinion of Mr Piozzi, let us converse no more, God bless you!

Johnson could not leave it at that, but his second letter was very different from his first.

London, 8th July, 1784

Dear Madam,

What you have done, however I may lament it, I have no pretence to resent, as it has not been injurious to me: I therefore breathe out one sigh more for tenderness, perhaps useless, but at least sincere.

I wish that God may grant you every blessing . . . and whatever I can contribute to your happiness I am very ready to repay, for that kindness which soothed twenty years of a life radically wretched. . . . The tears stand in my eyes. . . . I am with great affection . . .

In reply to this, Hester wrote him 'a very kind and affectionate farewell'; on 25 July she married Piozzi at Bath, and a month later they left England for

The end of the Age of Johnson: Lunardi's ascent from London in a balloon, September 1784. 'We now know a method of mounting into the air, and, I think, are not likely to know more . . . I had rather now find a medicine that can ease an asthma.'

France and Italy. It was a very happy marriage, which was to last twenty-five years.

Lord Thurlow's application to the King was unsuccessful, and though he himself offered to advance £600, Johnson declined it, and set off on his last journey to Ashbourne and Lichfield. His dropsy was getting worse, and on 29 October Anna Seward wrote, 'The great Johnson is here, labouring under the paroxysms of a disease which must speedily be fatal.' He stayed a few days with Hector at Birmingham, and with Adams at Oxford, before returning to Bolt Court on 16 November. A week later Fanny Burney called, and tactlessly asked if he had heard from Mrs Piozzi. 'No,' he cried, 'nor write to her. I drive her quite out of my mind. If I meet with one of her letters, I burn it instantly. I have burnt all I can find. I never speak of her, and I desire never to hear of her more.'

The last journey

Both his asthma and dropsy now became more violent. He slept little, and amused himself by translating Greek epigrams into Latin verse. He also composed a Latin inscription for Tetty's grave. On 8 December he made his will, leaving most of his estate to Francis Barber. His friends were constant visitors, among them Langton, Reynolds, Hawkins, Burke and Dr Burney. He was too ill to see Fanny, but sent a message: 'Tell Fanny to pray for me!'

When his dropsy was relieved from time to time by incisions to let out the fluid, he cried, 'Deeper! deeper!' and he deadened his pain with opium. But there came the time when Dr Brocklesby had to tell him that nothing but a miracle could save him. 'Then,' he said, 'I will take no more physic, not even my opiates: for I have prayed that I may render up my soul to God unclouded.' Yet he made one last desperate effort to prolong his life. On the morning of the 13th he took a pair of scissors and plunged them deep into the calf of each leg in an attempt to draw off the water, but he drew nothing but blood. He then fell into a doze. Francis and Mrs Desmoulins sat with him, and at about seven o'clock in the evening they noticed that the sound of his breathing had stopped. They went to look at him, and found he was dead.

A week later he was buried in Westminster Abbey, near the foot of Shakespeare's monument.

'Johnson is dead. Let us go to the next best. There is nobody; no man can be said to put you in mind of Johnson.' (*William Gerard Hamilton*)

BIBLIOGRAPHICAL NOTES

The Works of Samuel Johnson: with an Essay on his Life and Genius by Arthur Murphy, 12 vols., London, 1792. Many reprints.

The new Yale edition of the *Works* is in progress, 1958–.

The Rambler, Everyman ed.

Johnson's Dictionary: A Modern Selection, ed. E. L. McAdam and G. Milne, 1963.

Rasselas, ed. G. B. Hill, 1927.

Johnson on Shakespeare, ed. W. Raleigh, 1908.

A Journey to the Western Islands of Scotland and Boswell's *Journal of a Tour to The Hebrides*, ed. R. W. Chapman, 1924.

The Lives of the English Poets, 2 vols, Everyman ed.

The Poems, ed. D. N. Smith and E. L. McAdam, Oxford, 1941.

The Letters, ed. R. W. Chapman, 3 vols, 1952.

Johnson: Prose and Poetry, ed. M. Wilson, 1950.

Samuel Johnson: Selections (World's Classics), ed. R. W. Chapman, 1962.

J. Boswell, *The Life of Samuel Johnson*, ed. G. B. Hill, revised by L. F. Powell, 1934–40. (The standard edition, which includes *The Tour to the Hebrides*.)

The two-volume edition by R. Ingpen, 1925, is illustrated. Cheaper editions are the Oxford and Everyman.

J. Boswell, *The Journal of a Tour to The Hebrides with Samuel Johnson*, ed. from the MS. by F. A. Pottle and C. H. Bennett, 1936. There is an Everyman edition by L. F. Powell.

J. Hawkins, *The Life of Samuel Johnson*, 1787, ed. and abridged by B. H. Davis, 1962.

H. L. Piozzi, *Anecdotes of Samuel Johnson*, 1786, ed. S. C. Roberts, 1925.

Johnsoniana: or, Supplement to Boswell, London, 1836.

Johnsonian Miscellanies, ed. G. B. Hill, 1897, 1967.

L. Stephen, *Samuel Johnson*, 1878.

W. Raleigh, *Six Essays on Johnson*, Oxford, 1910.

A. M. Broadley, *Doctor Johnson and Mrs Thrale*, 1910.

Dr Johnson and Fanny Burney: being the Johnsonian Passages from the Works of Mme D'Arblay, ed. C. B. Tinker, 1912.

S. C. Roberts, *Doctor Johnson*, London, 1935.

C. E. Vulliamy, *Mrs Thrale of Streatham*, 1936.

J. W. Krutch, *Samuel Johnson*, New York, 1944.

J. L. Clifford, *The Young Samuel Johnson*, 1955.

M. A. Hopkins, *Dr Johnson's Lichfield*, London, 1956.

H. Pearson, *Johnson and Boswell*, London, 1958.

F. A. Pottle, *James Boswell: the Earlier Years, 1740–1769*, London, 1966.

Works by Johnson

Works about Johnson

CHRONOLOGY

1709 18 September N.S. Born at Lichfield, the son of Michael Johnson, bookseller.

1711 Touched for the 'King's Evil' by Queen Anne.

1716 Enters Lichfield Grammar School, under the headmastership of the 'wrong-headedly severe' John Hunter.

1725 Stays with his cousin Cornelius Ford.

1726 Leaves school and helps in his father's shop.

1728 October. Enters Pembroke College, Oxford.

1729 December. Poverty compels him to leave Oxford, without a degree.

1731 His father dies.

1732 Usher at Market Bosworth Grammar School.

1733 Translates *A Voyage to Abyssinia*.

1735 July. Marries Elizabeth Porter ('Tetty'), a widow aged forty-six.

1736 Sets up a private academy at Edial, near Lichfield.

1737 Goes to London with his pupil David Garrick.

1738 Begins to write for *The Gentleman's Magazine*, founded by Edward Cave. Publishes *London*, a satirical poem.

Friendship with Richard Savage. A period of great poverty.

1744 Publishes *The Life of Richard Savage*.

1745 *Miscellaneous Observations on the Tragedy of Macbeth*.

1747 Addresses his *Plan of a Dictionary* to the Earl of Chesterfield.

1748 Moves to 17 Gough Square, Fleet Street, where, with six assistants, he begins to compile his Dictionary.

1749 *The Vanity of Human Wishes*. Garrick produces Johnson's tragedy *Irene* at Drury Lane.

1750-2 *The Rambler*, a series of weekly essays (20 March 1750–14 March 1752).

1752 Tetty dies.

1754 Revisits Oxford, and meets Thomas Warton.

1755 Oxford University grants him an M.A. degree. Publication of his *Dictionary of the English Language*. At about this time he made new friends: Joshua Reynolds, Bennet Langton and Topham Beauclerk.

1756 *Proposals for a New Edition of Shakespear*; publication promised for Christmas 1757 (but eventually took place in 1765).

1758-60 *The Idler* essays.

1759 His mother dies, and he writes *Rasselas* to pay for her funeral.

1762 George III grants him a pension of £300 a year.

1763 16 May. Meets James Boswell, aged twenty-two, in Tom Davies's bookshop.

1764 The Literary Club formed.

1765 His edition of *Shakespeare's Plays* published.
Honorary Degree of LL.D., Trinity College, Dublin.
Meets Henry and Hester Thrale of Streatham, with whom he lives much of the time for the next sixteen years, talking rather than writing.
Takes a house in Johnson's Court, Fleet Street.

1769 Boswell introduces him to General Paoli.
Boswell married on 20 November and in Scotland until March 1772.

1773 August. Goes to the Hebrides with Boswell.

1774 April. Oliver Goldsmith dies.
July. Goes to Wales with the Thrales.

1775 Publishes *A Journey to the Western Islands of Scotland.*
Honorary degree of LL.D., Oxford University.
Goes to France with the Thrales.

1776 Moves to 8 Bolt Court, Fleet Street.
Takes Boswell to Oxford, Lichfield and Ashbourne.
Boswell tricks him into dining with John Wilkes.

1778 Beginning of friendship with Fanny Burney.

1779 Death of Garrick.

1781 *The Lives of the English Poets* published.
April. Henry Thrale dies.

1783 June. A stroke, and beginning of last illness.

1784 July. Breaks off friendship with Mrs Thrale when she announces her forthcoming marriage with Gabriele Piozzi.
13 December. Dies at Bolt Court, aged seventy-five.
20 December. Buried in Westminster Abbey.

ACKNOWLEDGEMENTS

The author is grateful to Mr K. K. Yung, Curator of the Johnson Birth-place Museum, to Miss Eliot of Dr Johnson's House, Gough Square, and to Mr Whitwell of Messrs Courage Barclay and Simonds for their help in obtaining illustrations, and to Miss Marian Berman and Mrs Dian Crawford-Johnson for their assembly and arrangement.

NOTES ON THE PICTURES

Frontispiece SAMUEL JOHNSON. Portrait sketch by Joshua Reynolds. Dr and Mrs T. E. Hanley Collection, Bradford, Pennsylvania.

4-5 LICHFIELD. The south-west prospect of the city. Engraving by S. and N. Buck, 1732. Map Room, British Museum.

6 LICHFIELD CATHEDRAL. Watercolour by Thomas Girtin, 1794. Thomas Girtin Collection. *Photo Royal Academy of Arts.*

7 JOHNSON'S BIRTHPLACE and St Mary's Church, Lichfield. Engraving by E. Finden after C. Stanfield.
MICHAEL JOHNSON. Engraving by E. Finden.

8 PETITION regarding the 'King's Evil', 1643. THE REBELLION of 1715. *The captured rebels returning to London.* Detail of an engraving by H. Terasson after Lud. Du Guernier. Department of Prints and Drawings, British Museum.

9 QUEEN ANNE. Portrait by J. Closterman. National Portrait Gallery, London.
GEORGE I. Portrait from the Studio of Kneller. National Portrait Gallery, London.

11 LICHFIELD GRAMMAR SCHOOL. Engraving by C. J. Smith after J. Buckler.

12 A MODERN MIDNIGHT CONVERSATION. Engraving by William Hogarth. Department of Prints and Drawings, British Museum.

13 THE BISHOP'S PALACE, Lichfield. The Entrance Front. *Photo Copyright Country Life.*

14 PEMBROKE COLLEGE, OXFORD. Engraving by Michael Burghers. Late seventeenth century. Bodleian Library, Oxford.

15 PEMBROKE COLLEGE, OXFORD. The Gateway. Engraving by E. Finden after C. Stanfield.

16-17 BIRMINGHAM. The east prospect of the city. Engraving by Harris after W. Westley, *c.* 1731. Map Room, British Museum.

18 SAMUEL JOHNSON. Engraving by E. Finden after a miniature worn by Mrs Johnson. Painted before 1752. Department of Prints and Drawings, British Museum.
JOHNSON'S MARRIAGE BOND, 1735. The Johnson Birthplace Museum, Lichfield.

19 PORTRAIT OF MRS JOHNSON. Hyde Collection, Somerville, New Jersey.

21 ADVERTISEMENT for the Edial Academy. From *The Gentleman's Magazine*, July 1736. EDIAL HALL, near Lichfield. Engraving by C. J. Smith.

22 GILBERT WALMESLEY'S LETTER to the Rev. Mr Colson, 1737. British Museum.

24 VIEW OF LONDON with St Paul's Cathedral and Wren's City churches. Engraving from Nouveau Théâtre de la Grande Bretagne 1729, vol. 4.

24-5 MAP OF LONDON, Westminster and Southwark, 1744. Map Room, British Museum.

25 THE IDLE 'PRENTICE EXECUTED AT TYBURN. Engraving by William Hogarth. Department of Prints and Drawings, British Museum.

GIN LANE. Engraving by William Hogarth, 1751. Department of Prints and Drawings, British Museum.

26 SECOND PAGE of Johnson's manuscript of *Irene*. Department of Manuscripts, British Museum. MS. Kings 306 f. 2.
A VIEW OF LONDON and Westminster from Greenwich Park, 1752. Engraving by Stevens. Department of Prints and Drawings, British Museum.

27 TITLE-PAGE from *The Gentleman's Magazine*, March 1738, with Johnson's first contribution in the Contents.
EDWARD CAVE. Engraving by E. Scriven after portrait by F. Kyte.

28 SOUTH-EAST VIEW of an old house in Sweedon's Passage, Grub Street, 1791. Engraving by J. T. Smith. Department of Prints and Drawings, British Museum.

29 THE FIRST PAGE of Johnson's *London*, 1738.

31 REPORT of a parliamentary debate by Johnson. From *The Gentleman's Magazine*, November 1741.

32 DAVID GARRICK as Richard III. Painting by William Hogarth. Walker Art Gallery, Liverpool.

33 WILLIAM WARBURTON. Portrait by C. Philips, between 1737 and 1747. National Portrait Gallery, London.

34 JOHNSON'S HOUSE, Gough Square. *Photo Brompton Studio.*

35 TITLE-PAGE of Johnson's *Plan of a Dictionary*, 1747.
PHILIP DORMER STANHOPE, 4th Earl of Chesterfield, *c.* 1742. Portrait by W. Hoare.
National Portrait Gallery, London.

36 A VIEW OF HAMPSTEAD from the Heath 1745. Engraving by W. H. Toms after Chatelain. Department of Prints and Drawings, British Museum.

37 IRENE. Miss Wallis as Aspasia. From John Bell's *British Theatre*, 1797. Raymond Mander and Joe Mitchenson Theatre Collection.

39 SIR JOHN HAWKINS. Engraving by R. Clamp after portrait by I. Roberts.
THE RAMBLER. First page of the first issue, 20 March 1750.

40 GRAVESTONE of Elizabeth Johnson. Bromley Parish Church. *Photo Brompton Studio.*

41 ANNA WILLIAMS. Portrait by Frances Reynolds formerly in the collection of James Boswell. Dr Johnson's House, Gough Square. *Photo Brompton Studio.*
FRANCIS BARBER. Portrait attributed to Reynolds's pupil, Northcote. Dr. Johnson's HOUSE, Gough Square. *Photo Brompton Studio.*

42 THOMAS WARTON. Engraving by E. Scriven after portrait by Joshua Reynolds.

43 DR JOHNSON IN THE ANTE-ROOM AT LORD CHESTERFIELD'S. Painting by E. M. Ward, 1845. The Tate Gallery, London.

44 TITLE-PAGE of the first volume of *A Dictionary of the English Language*, 1755.

45 FOUR ENTRIES from *A Dictionary of the English Language*, 1755.

46 JOSHUA REYNOLDS. Self-portrait. National Portrait Gallery, London.
FRANCES REYNOLDS. Mezzotint by S. W. Reynolds after portrait by Joshua Reynolds. Department of Prints and Drawings, British Museum.

47 BENNET LANGTON. Engraving after portrait by Joshua Reynolds. Department of Prints and Drawings, British Museum.
TOPHAM BEAUCLERK. Engraving by S. Bellin after portrait by G. P. Harding.

48 COVENT GARDEN MARKET, *c.* 1737. By B. Nebot. The Tate Gallery, London.
ST DUNSTAN'S in the West, Fleet Street, 1789. By Thomas Malton. Department of Prints and Drawings, British Museum.

49 BILLINGSGATE MARKET, 1762. Engraving by A. Vanhaecken. Department of Prints and Drawings, British Museum.
A VIEW OF NORTHUMBERLAND HOUSE, Charing Cross, looking west, and showing the Golden Cross Inn, 1753. Engraving after Canaletto. Department of Prints and Drawings, British Museum.

51 SAMUEL JOHNSON, 1756. Portrait by Joshua Reynolds. National Portrait Gallery, London.

52 THE IDLER. First page of the first volume, 1761.
TITLE-PAGE of Johnson's *Prince of Abissinia* (*Rasselas*), 1759.

53 HENRY FIELDING. Frontispiece, by William Hogarth, to Murphy's edition of Fielding's *Works*, 1762.
LAURENCE STERNE. Portrait in chalk and watercolour by L. C. de Carmontelle. National Portrait Gallery, London.
SAMUEL RICHARDSON, 1750. Portrait by J. Highmore. National Portrait Gallery, London.

54 OXFORD FROM THE NORTH. From J. Skelton's *Oxonia Antiqua*, 1823.
SOUTH FRONT of the Sheldonian Theatre. *Ibid.*

55 ENTRANCE TO JOHNSON'S HOUSE in Inner Temple Lane. Watercolour drawing by E. Findlay, 1855. Department of Prints and Drawings, British Museum.

56 GEORGE III, *c.* 1767. Portrait from the Studio of Allan Ramsay. National Portrait Gallery, London.

57 THE ENTRY ON 'TEA' from *A Dictionary of the English Language*, 1755.

59 THOMAS DAVIES'S SHOP, 8 Russell Street, Covent Garden. From G. W. Thornbury's *Old and New London*, 1873.

60 THOMAS DAVIES. Engraving by Schiavonetti after drawing by Hickey. Department of Prints and Drawings, British Museum.

61 JAMES BOSWELL, 1765. Portrait by George Willison. Scottish National Portrait Gallery, Edinburgh.

62 TEMPLE BAR, Fleet Street, 1796. By Thomas Malton. Department of Prints and Drawings, British Museum.

63 JOHNSON, GOLDSMITH AND BOSWELL at the Mitre Tavern, Fleet Street. Engraving by R. B. Parkes after the painting by Eyre Crowe.

64–5 GREENWICH HOSPITAL, *c.* 1748. Painting by Canaletto. National Maritime Museum, Greenwich.

65 OLIVER GOLDSMITH, *c.* 1770. Portrait from the Studio of Joshua Reynolds. National Portrait Gallery, London.

66–7 A LITERARY PARTY at Sir Joshua Reynolds's House. Engraving by W. Walker after the painting by James E. Doyle, who made careful reference to contemporary portraits. Dr Johnson's House, Gough Square. *Photo Brompton Studio.*

67 EDMUND BURKE, 1771. Portrait from the Studio of Joshua Reynolds. National Portrait Gallery, London.

68 CHARLES CHURCHILL. Portrait by J. S. C. Schaak. National Portrait Gallery, London.

69 LANGTON HALL, near Spilsby, Lincolnshire. From Howlett's *Views in the County of Lincoln*, 1800.

70 HENRY THRALE. Engraving by E. Scriven after the portrait by Joshua Reynolds.

71 MRS THRALE and her daughter, Hester ('Queeney'). Painting by Joshua Reynolds. Beaverbrook Art Gallery, Fredericton, New Brunswick.
STREATHAM PLACE. The house was demolished in 1863. Watercolour by W. H. Brooks. Dr Johnson's House, Gough Square. *Photo Brompton Studio.*

72-3 A VIEW ON THE HILL near the Five Mile Stone on the road to Streatham, 1782. Department of Prints and Drawings, British Museum.

73 THE SUMMER-HOUSE AT STREATHAM, 1773. Engraving by E. Finden after C. Stanfield.
JOHNSON'S HOUSE, Johnson's Court, Fleet Street. Engraving by E. Finden after J. Smith.

74 A VIEW OF THE EAST FRONT of the Queen's House, St James's Park, 1769. By J. Miller. Department of Prints and Drawings, British Museum.

75 THE EXHIBITION of the Royal Academy of Painting, 1771. By Charles Brandoin. Department of Prints and Drawings, British Museum.

76-7 A PERSPECTIVE VIEW of the Steyne at Brighton, 1778. Engraving by P. Mazell after I. Donowel. Department of Prints and Drawings, British Museum.

77 GARRICK AND THE SHAKESPEARE STATUE Painting by R. E. Pine. Courtesy of the Trustees and Guardians of Shakespeare's Birthplace, Stratford on Avon.
BOSWELL IN CORSICAN DRESS, as he appeared at the Shakespeare Jubilee in Stratford on Avon in 1769. Engraving by J. Miller after S. Wale. Dr Johnson's House, Gough Square. *Photo Brompton Studio.*

79 JOSEPH BARETTI. Engraving by J. Hardy after Joshua Reynolds. Dr Johnson's House, Gough Square. *Photo Brompton Studio.*
SAMUEL JOHNSON, *c.* 1769. Portrait by Joshua Reynolds. The Tate Gallery, London.
PASCAL PAOLI. Engraving by C. Bowles after portrait by Bembridge. Dr Johnson's House, Gough Square. *Photo Brompton Studio.*
JOHNSON'S LETTER TO MRS THRALE, 20 June 1771. The Johnson Birthplace Museum, Lichfield.

80 A CHOP HOUSE, with caricatures of Johnson and Boswell. Drawing by H. Bunbury. Department of Prints and Drawings, British Museum.
A COFFEE HOUSE in the early 1780s. Pen, ink and watercolour drawing by Thomas Rowlandson. Aberdeen Art Gallery.

81 OLD VAUXHALL GARDENS. In the supper-box, Johnson, Boswell, Mrs Thrale and Goldsmith. Pen, ink and watercolour drawing by Thomas Rowlandson. Alfred E. Pearson Collection. *Photo Royal Academy of Arts.*
A MASQUERADE SCENE in the Pantheon, 1773. Engraving by Charles White. Department of Prints and Drawings, British Museum.

82 THE CHURCH OF ST CLEMENT DANES, 1725. Engraving by John Kipp. Department of Prints and Drawings, British Museum.

83 GOLDSMITH'S DEDICATION TO JOHNSON, from the first edition of *She Stoops to Conquer*, 1773.

84 MRS BOSWELL. Portrait attributed to George Willison. Hyde Collection, Somerville, New Jersey. *Photo National Portrait Gallery, London.*

85 EAST VIEW OF EDINBURGH CASTLE, 1760. Engraving by Paul Sandby. Map Room, British Museum.
WALLACE NOOK, ABERDEEN, *c.* 1799. From J. C. Nattes: *Scotland*, 1804.

86–7 FOUR ILLUSTRATIONS from *The Picturesque Beauties of Boswell*, 1786, etched by Thomas Rowlandson after designs by Samuel Collings: 'Walking up the Highstreet', 'Tea', 'Chatting', 'Scottifying the Palate'.

86 JOHNSON IN TRAVELLING DRESS as described in Boswell's *Journal of a Tour to the Hebrides*. Engraving by T. Trotter. Department of Prints and Drawings, British Museum.

87 BEN NEVIS, INVERNESS-SHIRE. *Photo Robert M. Adam.*

89 FLORA MACDONALD. Portrait after Allan Ramsay. Scottish National Portrait Gallery, Edinburgh.
ILLUSTRATION FROM *The Picturesque Beauties of Boswell*, 1786, edited by Thomas Rowlandson after designs by Samuel Collings: 'Sailing among the Hebrides'.

90 LORD AUCHINLECK. Portrait by Allan Ramsay. From the Collection of Mr and Mrs Paul Mellon.

91 SAMUEL JOHNSON, *c.* 1773. Portrait by Joshua Reynolds. The Tate Gallery, London.
ILLUSTRATION FROM *The Picturesque Beauties of Boswell*, 1786, edited by Thomas Rowlandson after designs by Samuel Collings: 'The Contest at Auchinleck'.

92 THE GOLDSMITH MONUMENT, with Johnson's Latin epitaph. By Joseph Nollekens. South transept, Westminster Abbey. *Photo National Monuments Record.*

93 THE ROUND-ROBIN, a petition signed by Johnson's friends who wished him to write Goldsmith's epitaph in English.

94 ANNA SEWARD, 'The Swan of Lichfield'. Portrait by T. Kettle. National Portrait Gallery, London.

94–5 A VIEW OF DOVEDALE. Watercolour by Thomas Girtin. The Bacon Collection. *Photo Courtauld Institute of Art, London.*

95 SNOWDON, *c.* 1770. Painting by Richard Wilson. Walker Art Gallery, Liverpool.

97 JAMES MACPHERSON. Portrait after Joshua Reynolds. National Portrait Gallery, London.
THOMAS PERCY. Mezzotint by W. Dickinson after Joshua Reynolds. Department of Prints and Drawings, British Museum.

98–9 VIEW OF PARIS looking from the old grain market towards Pont Notre-Dame, 1782. Map Room, British Museum.

99 VIEW OF THE GATE OF ST DENIS, Paris. Aquatint by F. C. Lewis after Thomas Girtin. From *A Selection of Twenty of the Most Picturesque Views in Paris*, 1802. Department of Prints and Drawings, British Museum.

Notes

101 NO. 8 BOLT COURT, Fleet Street, London. Coloured drawing by C. Tomkins. Department of Prints and Drawings, British Museum.

102 SILHOUETTE OF LUCY PORTER, Johnson's stepdaughter. The Johnson Birthplace Museum, Lichfield.

102-3 THE LAKE, Blenheim Palace, Oxfordshire. *Photo Edwin Smith.*

103 RICHARD GREEN'S MUSEUM at Lichfield. Engraving by Cook after drawing by Stringer. Map Room, British Museum.

104-5 THE PUMP ROOM, Bath. From J. C. Nattes, *Bath Illustrated*, 1806.

105 JOHN WILKES. Engraving by William Hogarth. Department of Prints and Drawings, British Museum.

106 ASHBOURNE CHURCH, Derbyshire. Engraving by E. Finden after C. Stanfield.

107 JOSHUA REYNOLDS. Self-portrait as a deaf man, *c.* 1775. The Tate Gallery, London. SAMUEL JOHNSON, *c.* 1775. Portrait by Joshua Reynolds. Reproduced by courtesy of Courage Barclay and Simonds Ltd.

108 DR CHARLES BURNEY, 1781. Portrait by Joshua Reynolds. National Portrait Gallery, London.

109 FANNY BURNEY. Portrait by E. F. Burney. National Portrait Gallery, London.

111 THE GARRICK MONUMENT. By Henry Webber. South transept, Westminster Abbey, London. *Photo National Monuments Record.*

112 THE BURNING OF NEWGATE PRISON, 1 June 1780. Engraving by H. Roberts after O'Neil. Department of Prints and Drawings, British Museum.

JAMES BOSWELL. Engraving by E. Finden after George Langton.

112-13 GROSVENOR SQUARE. From James Malton, *A Picturesque Tour through the Cities of London and Westminster*, vol. II, 1792.

113 SOUTH FRONT OF THE ADELPHI. From Robert and James Adam, *Works in Architecture*, 1788-1822.

115 MRS THRALE'S BREAKFAST TABLE at the Brewery House in Southwark. Engraving by Barlow after Cruikshanks. From J. Merry, *Witticisms, Anecdotes, Jests and Sayings of Dr Johnson*, 1791.

116 THE SIGNATURES from the Deed of Sale of the Thrale Brewery, 1781. Reproduced by courtesy of Courage Barclay and Simonds Ltd.
THE ANCHOR BREWERY, Southwark. Painting by D. Wolstenholme. Reproduced by courtesy of Courage Barclay and Simonds Ltd.

117 LUTON HOO, Bedfordshire. The west front. *Photo A. F. Kersting.*

118 SAMUEL JOHNSON, 1782. Engraving by T. Trotter after J. Harding.

119 HESTER THRALE, 1781. Portrait by Robert Edge. Reproduced by courtesy of Courage Barclay and Simonds Ltd.
GABRIELE PIOZZI, 1793. Portrait by George Dance. National Portrait Gallery, London.

120 COWDRAY PARK, Sussex. Drawing, British Museum.

121 SAMUEL JOHNSON. Portrait by John Opie. *Photo National Galleries of Scotland, Edinburgh.* Reproduced by kind permission of the Earl of Crawford and Balcarres.

SALISBURY CATHEDRAL from the Bishop's Garden, 1826. Painting by John Constable. The Frick Collection, New York.

122 MRS SIDDONS as the Tragic Muse, 1784. Mezzotint and engraving after Joshua Reynolds.

123 DR WILLIAM ADAMS. Reproduced by permission of the Master and Fellows of Pembroke College, Oxford.

124 EDWARD THURLOW, 1806. Portrait by T. Phillips. National Portrait Gallery, London.

125 JAMES BOSWELL, 1786. Portrait by Joshua Reynolds. National Portrait Gallery, London.

127 VIEW OF THE ASCENT of Lunardi's air-balloon from the artillery ground, 15 September 1784. Engraving by T. Deeble. Department of Prints and Drawings, British Museum.

128 MONUMENT TO SAMUEL JOHNSON. By John Bacon, 1796. St Paul's Cathedral, London. *Photo National Monuments Record.*

INDEX

Date Due

MY 3 '78